Praise for **A Life**

"These stories are raw and humorous, b
reads this book will take away a ton of n
salespeople to, 'Eat, Sleep and Prospect
the scars and bank account to prove it. Do y

—**Jeb Blount**, CEO Sales Gravy, Inc., bestselling author & keynote

"I've known Joe for many years. He writes and coaches from a place of experience
and truth. It's rare that you see a book from a master salesperson and sales
leader that is this revealing and honest. I can't think of a salesperson or leader
that wouldn't read this and come away with a dozen new tools to apply to
their business. Joe's followed The CAP Equation with another gem!"

—**Andy Glaub**, senior V.P.; director of Aflac U.S. sales

"A Life in Sales, Volume I is a revealing and refreshing look into Joe Buzzello's early sales
career. Joe holds nothing back as he recounts all of the fear, doubt and call reluctance
that crept into his head as he began selling. As the subtitle guarantees, Joe learned
much from the 'mentors,' 'sinners' and 'saints' that crossed his path. I learned and
laughed, and you will too! This is a great read for those of us that LOVE this game."

—**Bill Cates**, CSP, CPAE, author and hall of fame speaker,
founder Referral Coach International

"I've thought very highly of Joe Buzzello's writing over the years, and this
book may represent his best work yet. In this volume Joe speaks to the basic
elements of success, those simple truths that some people starting out may
simply overlook. He took massive ownership and responsibility for his sales
career and invested himself fully in the work. These are high impact stories
and lessons—a tremendous read for any entrepreneur or sales pro!"

—**Leeza Carlone Steindorf**, speaker, trainer, mediator–Tony Robbins Results
Coach, award winning author of *Connected Parent, Empowered Child*

"I love war stories shared by our American heroes who have willingly put
themselves in harm's way to defend the freedoms we all enjoy. But I also love the
'war stories' shared from the mouths of our heroes in sales who've faced rejection,
call reluctance, and fluctuating income, but still persevered to become hugely
successful. Joe Buzzello is one of those heroes." A Life In Sales is filled with
thought provoking stories. They're massively entertaining! Great job, Joe!"

—**Jeff C. West**, award-winning author of the heartwarming
business fable, *The Unexpected Tour Guide*

"As a branding expert, I can tell you that Joe's brand is all about being real. Joe uses his
genuine sales and entrepreneurial experiences to paint pictures you will easily become
immersed in. He doesn't hold anything back as he invites you inside of his early struggles
and lessons. It was wonderful to trace his path in this book from a lack of self-esteem
and career uncertainty, to confidence, and then much higher levels of success."

—**S. Renee**, self-esteem & branding expert, image consultant, speaker, author, coach

"What's fun about this book is the unfiltered voice Joe uses as he unwinds his early sales and leadership experiences. However, what is ultimately more valuable for the reader are those lessons outlined at the end of each chapter. Those lessons are golden! This is a great read."

—**John Grubbs**, best selling author, Leading The Lazy

"Joe's certainly had a Hall of Fame career. He's impacted many lives while in leadership roles. However, his work after being in the corporate game has had just as much of an impact. In Joe's long form writing, he's been able to capture those seminal moments when a mentor, saint or sinner walked into his path and permanently altered his way of thinking. Put this book on your 'must read' list!"

—**Adam Michaels**, V.P., west territory director, Aflac

"Joe has devoted his life to sales excellence and organizational development. His latest book, A Life In Sales, Volume I, takes you through his very early struggles. Anyone that has spent a day in commission sales will identify with these experiences. This book will also resonate with entrepreneurs—the kind of people that have taken the leap of faith into the great unknown. Simply a great read—packed with learning moments!"

—**Marc Emmer**, president, Optimize, Inc. – author, Momentum: How Companies Decide What to Do Next

"A Life In Sales is jammed full of completely relatable stories re-told by a master salesperson. The book is incredibly riveting and entertaining. I also learned a great deal from Joe B.'s invaluable insights and perspectives on the sales game. He knows what it really takes to WIN!"

—**Alex Bayer**, CEO, Genius Juice

"I like a story that outlines the real struggles a person faces on their way to success. In Volume I of Joe's work, A Life In Sales, he gives us a taste of those early hurdles. He carefully explains how he utilized solid mentorship to alter his actions and thinking to create success in his life and career. This is a great read for anyone that wants to transition from where they're at currently, to a place of higher achievement and service. I know a lot about Joe's success story. There are more saints and sinners to follow in his life. I can't wait for Volume II to be released!"

—**Dr. Tommy Watson**, America's leading expert on turning transitions into success

"Joe is a tour guide, not a travel agent. He's taken the trip and knows every aspect of the journey. His ability to draw real life lessons from his experiences is the best I've seen. Joe is an amazing storyteller and he'll keep you interested and learning at the same time."

—**Les Heinsen**, founder, Element 79 Vineyards

"It's crazy to read this book and learn that Joe's original sales training took place in the late '70's and early '80's. This book is a wonderful reminder that greatness doesn't happen overnight. I've always thought it would be awesome to go back in time and pick Joe's brain during different stages of his career. These pages allowed me to hop into my imaginary DeLorean and watch one of the greatest sales leaders in the industry transform into the master that he is."

—**Chad P. Schneider**, director, channel sales, JellyVision

"The stories are surreal—like reading a movie script. While the stories are cool, it's the powerful lessons that make the book a great read. There are so many pertinent instructions that a salesperson or leader would HAVE to grow personally after digesting this book. This is one of those 100% must-reads for B2B sales professionals.

—**Jack Holder**, insurance industry thought leader

"As the founder of a non profit that benefits fatherless boys, we stress values such as integrity, the willingness to take action and personal responsibility. If you read about Joe's early career as a salesperson, it's all there. He searched out mentors and listened to them. He became a good follower, and eventually a young, dynamic leader. I have known Joe for just over a decade, so I met him after he was a self-made millionaire. I didn't know the fine details of his early career. A Life in Sales, Volume I, shines a light on Joe's early battles. I actually can't wait for Volume II.

—**Jason Hill**, founder & CEO, Young Warriors

"Throw away your corporate training books and learn directly from the sage! Joe B. has captured his very best cocktail stories in a meaningful way. The lessons are as ageless as the photograph on the front cover. A must read for any salesperson who wants to turn their career into a legacy."

—**Captain Doug Fox**, founder/CEO, FoxysCustomCruises.com, "The captain that makes it happen"

"Whether you're green as can be or already a proven rock-star commission sales pro, you're going to love this book! From the story of Joe's first day on the car lot to the explanation of his 'accidental' career in the insurance business, he draws you in and you'll surely relate. While many of Joe's stories had me cracking up, there's also a deep and intelligent side to his book that will certainly help catapult your sales growth. By the time you're finished with the first chapter, you'll quickly realize that learning is what Joe's primary focus was and how he genuinely wants his readers to come away with a few golden nuggets."

—**Eric Silverman**, bestselling author of Breaking Through The Status Quo - 2017 EBA Voluntary Advisor of the Year

"As a fellow master sales trainer and speaker, I have enjoyed and respected Joe's transparency. This book and the stories from the early part of his sales career gives the reader some genuine insights into what true salesmanship is all about, and how he formed key paradigms that launched a remarkable career and personal wealth. Joe is real, the stories are real and the lessons are real. Thanks for sharing, Joe!"

—**Paul Schween**, public seminar promoter, author, speaker and master sales trainer

"Joe has that rare gift of good storytellers. When I originally read his stories, I found myself connecting to my life's stories in ways that made the lessons they contained more personal and meaningful. The unique format of this book helped me reap more value than I could have ever gotten from simply a principles based guide, or a typical 'how to' book on sales and entrepreneurial success. The fact that his stories are so entertaining as well makes this book a must read."

—**Bill Leider**, managing partner, Axies Group, a consulting firm focused on creating life-changing transformational leadership

"I have witnessed Joe become an accomplished salesperson, leader, speaker and author, but it wasn't always that way. When I first met Joe I would have described his sales technique as that of a Greyhound. Once the rabbit was released he ran very hard and fast to catch it. Over the last forty years, I have trained him to be more of a spectator, focused on the entire race versus just catching the rabbit. Like Joe's waistline, his knowledge of sales and leadership has grown exponentially under my tutelage. He truly has moved from being in the profession of sales to being a true professional salesperson—a true master, and he has me to thank for that."

—**Gary Ware**, founder & president, Ware Group General Agencies

"Joe has chosen to share some very personal stories that provide a great road map of thinking. These lessons are based on experiences that were both good and bad and that's what makes this book such a great read."

—**Tim Martin,** founder, SuccessIsVoluntary.com

"You had me at Chapter 11, 'Spaghetti Logic.' The rest of the book is 'gravy,' a wonderful collection of methods and mindsets that clearly and accurately define the art of selling and what it takes to be a superstar!"

—**Anthony Parinello,** Wall Street Journal, best-selling author, Selling to VITO, the Very Important Top Officer

A LIFE IN
SALES

A LIFE IN SALES

Mentors, Saints & Sinners –
Wisdom, Truths & Lies and
The Incredible Lessons Learned

VOLUME 1:
The Stone Age 1978–1982

JOE BUZZELLO

Author of the sales training classic, **The CAP Equation**

ISBN: 978-0-9969503-1-2

To Beth Buzzello
I honestly wouldn't know what I'd be
without you, right by my side.

CONTENTS

Not a Sequel

The concept for this book came about quite unintentionally.

I published my first non-fiction book, *The CAP Equation*, in February 2015. That book was quite intentional. It breaks down and distills a foolproof sales process, one that is easily learned and duplicated. There were a few interesting stories told in that book, but not that many. I was somewhat economical with my sidebar tales. I didn't want to write a behemoth manuscript. I knew that people wouldn't read a book from a first time author if it was too fat. My wife reminds me that most salespeople have the attention span of a toy poodle anyway.

Based on my own attention span, I think she may have nailed that one.

It was strange to me that the *stories* in that first book were the parts most recalled and commented on. I didn't think that would be the case. I thought I would lose people's attention with too many inside tales. My editor told me the same thing, in so many words. I wasn't certain she was 100% right, but you pay professional editors thousands of dollars to clean up your work, so you tend to listen to them after you pay them.

Hence, I withheld a ton of great stories from that first book.

I followed up *The CAP Equation* with a novel based on actual events. *Drawing Circles* was one BIG story, a fictionalized version of a particular experience that rocked me to my core at an early age. In that book I used one narrow piece of my background as the platform for some phenomenal characters and an unbelievable storyline about greed and abuse of trust.

Since these two books were published, I've been out on the road speaking and training. If you've been out on that long lonely highway, then you know it's quite common to sit around after a meeting or event and have a cocktail or two...or three. The really juicy stories start to flow after the truth serum is served up. Someone would ask, "Hey Joe, you mentioned that your first job in sales was selling cars at a Ford dealership in North Hollywood in the '70s...you were seventeen, right? What the hell was that like?"

It would be like someone pulled the chord on a Chatty Cathy doll. I'd unwind the story.

The thing you have to understand about stories is that most people don't volunteer the really good ones right up front. They hold them back until they believe they're actually going to be heard and understood. There's nothing worse than baring your soul only to have the listener get up, or switch conversations, or lose context.

This never happened as we sat around late night after an event. Nobody was ever bored when I'd tell about this stuff!

Maybe it was the liquor.

I'd begin telling the stories about Universal Ford, "The Home of Low Prices." People's jaws would drop open as I recounted the sales tactics they taught their salespeople, some legal, most not so legal. They'd also ask me about when I was selling those $39.00 accident plans for Pennsylvania Life, walking into sixty-plus doors a day, cold calling, making only $19.50 per sale. They'd ask, "How the hell did you even survive?" I would tell them about hiring 400 salespeople and having 397 of them quit.

And then I quit.

I'd tell some of the sordid tales surrounding my involvement in the Amway business—the crap that went on there during the '80s. I'd recount how my upline Diamond (and best friend), wound up getting his butt sent to federal prison for four years. They'd ask about my long career with the company that has the spokes-duck. The stories and characters from my Aflac career are so rich and plentiful that I suppose they'd fill up a volume all on their own—and most likely will. (Hint, hint)

As my fables told around our cocktail campfire unraveled, people listening would always circle back to the rich lessons woven into the experiences. They'd pick out specific incidents and make comments like, "So that's where you got that catch phrase you always use." Or they'd ask, "So how did that episode change you?" As *last call* was yelled out, I'd usually mumble something like, "Hey, it's been *real*, but I gotta' get to bed." Then somebody would always suggest something like, "Hey, Joe B., you have to put this stuff in a book—these stories—they're crazy good."

I'd agree.

And then I'd go to sleep.

After a few years of people telling me to "publish those damn stories" I began to feel compelled to record the historical and hysterical events on paper. As I started to do this, something really cool happened. All of the mentors, characters, detractors, criminals, demons, saints, wisdoms, lies and truths came roaring back to me.

It all flooded back into my noggin like a tsunami of emotions. Most of the recollections made me smile. A few choked me up. The likeness of people I hadn't thought about in three or four decades came back to haunt me a little. I guess you were wrong mom... smoking weed in the '70s didn't make me forget stuff! LOL!

This exercise also helped me recall what I was feeling and thinking at the time of the events and experiences. It was more than a little bit astonishing to soak in the vibrant recall, but I think I know what happened here.

When you read and/or write, you have to use unusual parts of your cognitive imagination to paint a complete picture. When you listen to an audio or watch a video, a lot of the cerebral work is already done for you. Sounds and images are pushed at you—you don't have to use as much of your ingenuity. When all you have are words on paper, you have to dig deep, use your God-given creativity and craft all of those sights and sound bites for yourself.

There is a reward for doing this.

As I went deep into the crevices of my mind in an effort to pull out the stuff I'd need to reiterate a story, more than I bargained for appeared. I rediscovered where and when I'd formed a few of my treasured philosophies. On more than one occasion, during the first drafts of this book, I'd think, "Yeah...that's where I learned that—that's when I began to feel that way."

Something else hit me as I began to sort through all of these rich stories and experiences. There was far too much content for just one book. I'd have to break my long sales career into separate volumes.

So, here's the first iteration of *A Life In Sales–Mentors, Saints & Sinners,–Wisdom, Truths & Lies, and The Incredible Lessons Learned*

This is Volume I–The Stone Age, 1978–1982.

Volume I encompasses the early years of my sales career, 1978 – 1982. I refer to this as "the stone age" because we *sold* and *lived* with ZERO technology. There were only three primary channels on my television set. A computer was something that filled a large room in some big corporation's temperature controlled basement. If you wanted to research something, you drove to a public library. If you wanted to find an address you had to open up your big, bulky Thomas Brother's map for L.A. County. If you were on the road and wanted to call someone, you had to drive around until you found a payphone.

Then you had to hope you had a few dimes in your pocket! LOL!

Once you did call someone, you had to pray that you didn't get a busy signal. If they weren't home, you hoped they were cool enough to have an answering machine with an empty cassette tape inside.

In 1978, most people weren't that cool!

You just had to keep calling them back.

So...this was the stone age.

This first volume of work focuses on how I wound up getting into the game of selling and how my early experiences formed the basis of my philosophies in sales.

Now, before you contact me and ask if all of these experiences REALLY happened, or if these characters are *real* people, the answer is YES. I'm not sure why, but I seem to have the knack of getting into unusual places with some pretty unconventional people. I didn't change any names to protect the innocent in this volume of work. I didn't feel the need to. Many of these people are long retired or long gone anyway.

I want you to understand that it's my intense desire to do MORE than just tell you a good story. You will note that at the end of many of the chapters in this book I tap the brakes—slow you down and supply you with a short list of incredible lessons. These are the learning moments I took away from the experiences. I hope you can draw from these lessons as well.

So, this is **not exactly a sequel** to *The CAP Equation*.

This book takes you a few levels deeper into the stories, the real genuine characters, my psyche, etc.

I've spent my life in sales.

These are some of the early stories.

You are invited to learn something from them.

Joe Buzzello

At our new home in Scottsdale, Arizona – Winter 2018

CHAPTER ONE

A Real Job

"The first duty of a human being is to assume the right functional relationship to society— more briefly, to find your real job, and do it."

—CHARLOTTE PERKINS GILMAN, Writer

When your tougher than nails, WWII veteran father looks you square in the eyes and says, "Son, it's time for you to get a *real* job," and he doesn't even bother to remove the Camel non-filter cigarette from between his lips, you know he's damn serious.

In late June 1978, I had just graduated from Grant High School in North Hollywood, California. All of my friends were off to college. I'd enjoy one last summer of debauchery with them, and then their paths would lead out of the San Fernando Valley.

Mine would not.

My high school grades were horrendous. I did nothing to prepare for college; I had a hard time focusing in the classroom and had no interest in anything other than golf and fine art. Golf would have been my ticket to a higher education if I hadn't gotten into an altercation with the golf coach during my senior year. That little scuffle got me kicked off the team, which is clearly a story for another time. The miniscule amount of money my parents had set aside for college tuition would be used to buy a yellow AMC Matador and two business suits. The suits were from J.C. Penney, one of them was powder blue, and the other was dark brown. Whatever *real job* interview I could talk myself into would be driven to in that yellow Matador, and I'd surely be wearing one of those sexy new suits along with my white dress shoes.

My father, nicknamed Buzz, had been crystal clear in his message to me. My part-time job as night manager at Valley Beverage Liquors would not "cut the mustard" whatever the hell that meant. He methodically opened the *The Valley News* to the classified section of that shitty newspaper and placed it on the kitchen table. He sat my ass down and handed me a red, felt tip pen to circle any possible jobs. He wasn't leaving anything to chance. I scanned the newspaper and flipped the pages as the newsprint ink soaked into my sweaty fingertips. Surfing the Internet would have been easier, but it would be many years before Al Gore would invent the World Wide Web, so this was my primary job search tool. Even at the tender age of seventeen, I had a loathing for manual labor, so I eliminated many of the pages in the thick classified section. My attention was drawn to the section marked, "SALES."

I wasn't the most outgoing guy in the world. The two things I did well were hit a golf ball and create pen and ink drawings. I was an accomplished artist at a young age, but didn't know how to make a buck doing that. Both of those skills, golf and art, were solitary activities. It was okay with me to be referred to as a "loner." That said, my close friends had told me they thought I'd make a good salesperson. They'd say things like, "You like to debate issues," or stuff like, "Once you get an idea in your head, you don't let it go, you like to convince people to do things." So with that random counsel in mind, I focused on the largest ad featured in the sales section.

It read:

Join the Universal Ford sales team and make people's dreams come true. Universal Ford, The Home of Low Prices! Sales positions now available. No experience necessary!

I liked cars and I didn't think selling them would be that hard. The one line at the bottom of the ad sounded good to me, *"No experience necessary!"* In fact, that line described me perfectly! I circled the ad with that red felt tip pen, walked over to our big black rotary phone and dialed the number. The receptionist put me through to a guy who spoke with a thick French Canadian accent. His name was Serge Arsenault. He asked me a few questions (but damn few), and then he invited me in for an interview. The next morning I put on my powder blue suit and drove that yellow AMC Matador to the dealership on Lankersheim Boulevard. I don't remember much of the interview, but I do recall it was short. After about ten minutes of chitchat and bullshit questions, Serge stuck out his hand and announced, "You're hired. Go down 'dere to da Van Nuys DMV and apply for your sales license. Call me when you have it in your hands, yeah?"

Upon my return home I advised Buzz that his son officially had a *real* job. He smiled proudly and winked at me while sitting in his big brown vinyl recliner, watching a Star Trek rerun on channel 5, never bothering to remove the eternal Camel non-filter from his lips. A week later I had the automobile sales license in my hand. I called Serge and told him I'd received the license in the mail. In that humorous Pepé Le Pew accent he yelled, "Beautiful. Get your ass in here da day after tomorrow…at NOON, yeah? You got some paper-work to do and 'den you're on da line at 1:00—second shift."

I wasn't sure what "on da line" meant, and it was difficult to follow everything he was saying, because he talked so funny, but two days later I showered, shaved, put on my powder blue suit again and drove my AMC Matador to the lot. I was careful to park down the street because I wasn't driving a Ford. I found Serge in his little office on the south side of the main showroom. He was sitting in a cloud of smoke with paperwork swarming over his small desk. The leaning tower of files looked like they were ready to tumble onto the floor at the slightest movement. He glanced up, without bothering to stand, and he shook my hand. "Joel, welcome to da Universal Ford sales family, home of da low prices."

I felt obliged to correct him on my butchered first name, so I politely replied, "It's 'Joe,' Mr. Arsenault." He looked at me, half annoyed, half apologetic and mumbled, "Yeah, right…Joe. Sit your-self down 'dere."

Within a few minutes I had signed my name to a bunch of stuff I didn't read. After finishing that, Serge handed me a small box. I opened it and inside were several hundred shiny pieces of cardboard. I carefully removed one of the cards and stared at it. I'd never seen anything so beautiful in my life. There was my name, spelled cor-rectly, with the title, "SALES REPRESENTATIVE" below it. The Universal Ford sign was pictured to the left of my name. I'm not sure, but I think violins and trumpets were playing in my head.

Serge broke the spell.

"Hey, kid, put a few of dose in your pocket and follow me, yeah. Time to hit da line."

I was about to break the seal on a sales career that would last over forty years. My life in sales would create great wealth for me; the wealth I'm referring to would come in many forms. Of course, I didn't know all of that the time. I just knew that I had a business card with my name on it, and Buzz was happy that I'd found a *real* job.

THE INCREDIBLE LESSONS

Nothing earth shattering here, however there is one *subtle* lesson I can point to. It's about the people in your life that care about you.

✓ **Everyone needs a PUSH at some point in his or her life.**

My dad's gentle nudge—the newspaper and red pen—was the catalyst I needed to circle a job listing and make a phone call. If somebody cares enough about you to **encourage you** to take some action in your life, or they love you enough to **challenge you** to think or behave differently, **cherish that person.**

Not many of these caring people come around in our short lives.

CHAPTER TWO

Losing My Sales Virginity

We walked out to the furthest part of the lot and approached a sales rep that was standing there like a damn statue. He was on the prey for a prospect. I guessed that he was a few years older than me, probably early twenties. He wore what appeared to be an expensive suit, definitely not from J.C. Penney. His hair was oiled down and slicked back.

"Frankie, dis is Joel Bazallero. Show him da ropes. You two will get along good. You're both Spanish, yeah?"

With that bizarre introduction, the slaughtering of my entire Christian name and the mistaken identification of both of our national origins, Serge just turned and walked away.

After Serge was out of earshot, I advised Frankie of my *actual* name, and then informed him I was Italian American. We had a good laugh at how oblivious Serge was to some very basic shit. Frankie was born in Mexico and his family immigrated to Los Angeles. He had been at Universal Ford for nine months.

After nine months he was considered a grizzled veteran.

He wanted to move up in the ranks, so he had volunteered to break in a few of the new guys, show them how to work the line. A liner's job was to make sure prospects were never alone as they walked onto the lot and started looking at window stickers. Frankie explained that everybody started at Universal Ford as, "a liner." Liners were to be positioned at the place where the asphalt met the sidewalk bordering Lankersheim Boulevard. Universal Ford had an "UP" system. This meant that the liners were supposed to take turns being, "UP to bat" as prospects drove up to the curb. I soon learned that taking polite turns to be UP didn't always happen.

Frankie told me to, "Watch and learn." After we had been standing there for a few minutes making small talk and sweating bullets in the summer heat, a couple drove up in a gold Ford Fairlane Sedan. There was another liner much closer to where the couple was parking, but that wasn't going to deter Frankie. He quickly moved over and repositioned himself right smack in front of where they'd have to exit their car. The other liner, an older guy that wasn't on our team, just shook his head in disgust and walked away. Frankie was, apparently, the alpha dog in that mix, or the old guy just plain had no fight in him.

Or both.

The husband had a newspaper tucked under his arm as he exited his vehicle. Frankie whispered to me, "This one's a 'mooch'. He's coming in on the advertised special." I had no idea what "mooch," meant, but I smiled, nodded and kept my mouth shut. The prospect spoke first to Frankie.

"Hello, young man. I want to look at the advertised special...the '78 Fairmont. Can you show it to me?"

Frankie smiled. He had more big white teeth in his mouth than

I'd ever seen before or since. He stuck out his hand and said, "Yes, sir. That's a great car." Frankie started chatting the couple up. On the walk over to the ad special he asked them if they had any kids. They did have a son and Frankie asked what high school he'd attended. It was the same one he went to and he seemed to recognize their son's name. He told them their son was a popular guy on campus. The mother smiled and Frankie kept the conversation going. "Boy, you guys are lucky that the advertised special is still here on the lot. A lot of people have looked at it today, but nobody's bought it yet. I thought for sure that somebody would have snapped it up by now. Seems like a fine car to me. Come on...let's look inside."

The couple was eager to see the car. They were bouncing along behind us, but you could tell that Frankie had started the husband's wheels turning. We walked to what must have been the hottest part of the lot, the location that was in direct sunlight all day. There sat the advertised special, in all of its glory. It was an unsightly chocolate brown color, it had plain-Jane aluminum hubcaps and the manual windows were rolled up tight. The interior was black vinyl and there was an empty space where an AM/FM stereo cassette deck should have been. The wires were actually sticking out of the hole in the dash. My first thought was "what idiot ordered this car for sales inventory?" The second question in my head was, "who decided this ugly piece of crap should be the featured advertised special?" It didn't make any sense at all to me at that point.

The newspaper was still sticking out from under the husband's arm, folded open to the page with our ad, so I glanced at the price. It was several thousand dollars lower than ANY other Fairmont we had passed on the lot. The price was ridiculously low—probably below the dealer's cost, I thought. The car looked to be stripped down to the bare minimum equipment, and the interior was as atrocious as the exterior. Then it hit me—even before Frankie opened up the suffocating sweatbox and motioned for the husband to get in... they didn't want to sell this car! This car was a magnet...a loss leader, a vehicle priced so low in the paper that anybody in the market for a brand new Ford couldn't resist coming down to check it out.

What happened next was hysterical.

Frankie jacked open both front doors and persuaded the husband and wife to get inside. I have to tell you, it can get well above 100 degrees on many days during a summer in the San Fernando Valley, and it was at least 95 degrees on this particular day. So, with all four windows rolled up and the black vinyl seats radiating heat, the inside temperature must have been about ten degrees hotter than the surface of the sun. The couple lasted about three seconds in the car. They both popped out like springs were attached to their rear ends. The husband blurted out, "It's pretty warm in there young man." Then he requested, "Why don't you start up the car and crank on the AC, son?"

Frankie smiled his big smile. That's exactly what he wanted to hear.

Frankie grabbed the keys from above the visor. He looked into the car, then dramatically rubbed his forehead and frowned. He turned to the husband and in a dramatic, contrite tone asked, "Were you nice folks looking for a Fairmont with an air conditioner?"

I watched this bullshit dance unfold with mixed emotions—a morbid fascination of the incredibly effective tactics, but I also felt slightly sickened by the manipulative nature of it all. It didn't seem very fair or honest to me. The husband looked at his wife and meekly asked, "We do need an AC, don't we honey?" She nodded her head and assured him they couldn't drive around the Valley in a car that doesn't have an air conditioner.

Frankie had them in the palm of his hand and he didn't miss a beat.

"No problem folks. By the way, what color car did you have your heart set on today?" The couple said that gold was their favorite color. Frankie picked up the baton and ran with it. "That's a great color. My favorite too! Let's go into the nice cool showroom...get out of this darn heat. I'm going to have my manager find us a gold

Fairmont with an air conditioner on the lot. He'll have a lot boy drive it up so you can look at it. Come on with me folks."

Frankie led them into the showroom like the pied piper, continuing to pepper them with questions about their son—if he'd attended college, what work he was now doing, etc. Mom and dad were gushing about their boy; they couldn't stop talking about him as he led them into a small cubicle that was referred to as a, "box." Two hours later the couple drove off the lot in their brand new, fully loaded, 1978 Gold Ford Fairmont Deluxe. Incidentally, the car had an air conditioner, a stereo and almost every option imaginable... and they'd paid close to full price for the vehicle.

There was a definite sales process at Universal Ford, Home of Low Prices. The newest salespeople lined up on Lankersheim Boulevard. The liners took their turn being "up to bat." The liner would show their "UP" (prospect) the advertised special, if that was what they said they were coming to see. Then, the liner would sell them OFF of the advertised car. They'd use the advertised special to determine what colors and options the prospect really wanted. Then the liner would tell them that the very same car might be on the showroom floor or close by. Then they would lure them into the showroom and get them to sit down in a small cubicle type office while they located the car. This was referred to as "boxing" the prospect. Frankie explained to me that boxing a prospect was the most critical part of the process because the prospect would then be ensnared into a controlled environment. It would be much harder for them to turn and walk off the lot and the final piece of the puzzle, the "closer" would make sure of that.

As soon as a prospect was boxed, the liner would get a convenient page over the loud speaker that they had a phone call waiting. The liner would introduce their prospect to a closer, usually their direct manager, like Serge. The liner would go chase another prospect while the closer would nail down a rough price, or an approximate monthly payment that the prospects were willing to spend on the car of their dreams. When the closer had a summary commitment from the prospect, he would tell them they were locating the car—cooling it off and driving it up.

At this juncture the real fun and games would begin.

The closer would ask the prospect about their trade-in—would they like a "great price" on their old car? Predictably, the prospect was always curious as to what they could get for their old bucket of bolts. They'd hand over their keys in an instant and the closer would also ask where the vehicle's registration was, and it was usually in the glove compartment.

Viola!

You get it, right?

Now the prospect couldn't leave the dealership. They were stranded—no keys or registration! That's why it was so important to box the prospect. Frankie instructed me that, "Once they're sitting down in the box, talking trade-in, they're toast—they're virtually closed."

I quickly learned that Universal Ford was a, "T.O. house." That meant that a liner would "turn over" a prospect to another salesperson on their team if they were losing control. They were to signal one of their teammates. The teammate would walk over, tell the liner that they had an urgent call waiting and then take over the conversation. If your manager found out you didn't turn over a prospect and they walked off the lot, you could be fired.

Frankie continued explaining what happened when a prospect was in the box. The closer would take the prospect's ridiculously low offer (and their keys) into the general manager's office, saying something like, "The big boss is not going to like this offer. He's going to throw me out. But you're nice people, so I'm going to go to work for you." It was a classic good cop, bad cop thing. The closer's job was simply to get some kind of price commitment, a small deposit and the keys to their trade-in. The general manager was the wizard behind the curtain. He was a dude named, Al Boegner.

After the closer went back and forth to the general manager's office a dozen times, they'd either meet at a price the prospect agreed was fair (usually just below full sticker price) or the prospect would be so worn out, they'd simply roll over and give up. Some prospects would become angry with all the back and forth, which could take hours. Sometimes they'd walk out of the showroom in a huff. The closer would apologize, tell them he'd done his best and he was also upset that "the big manager wouldn't budge." However, the closer wouldn't chase after the prospects. He didn't have to. He'd sit back down in the box and light up a smoke.

He knew they'd be back.

The prospects would walk to where their car was originally parked, but it wasn't there anymore. The used car manager had moved it during the appraisal process. They'd hide the prospect's car behind the service bays. Even if the prospect found their car, which rarely happened, they still had no keys. If the prospect did go back there and ask for the keys, the service manager was trained to shrug his shoulders and say, "They must be in the showroom." In the odd event that the prospects found their car, and the used car manager was sloppy enough to leave the keys in it, the prospects would drive off, but soon remember that they didn't have their vehicle registration. Their registration was sitting in the file of offers and counter offers.

After five or ten minutes of searching for their car, the prospect would usually march back into the showroom. The closer would calm them down; tell them that the car was most likely "moved" by the used car department for the appraisal. He'd ask the receptionist to get them a cup of coffee while he located the car. After a couple of minutes the closer would appear with a friendly smile. He'd explain that the used car manager felt so bad that he's having the lot boy wash their car for them. The closer would then show up and shout, "Great news!" He'd tell them he made one more trip to the, "Big boss's office." Then he'd lay it on thick. "I told him what happened with your trade-in—the confusion—he felt bad that you were upset.

I've never seen him do this…he's going to knock down the price real close to your last offer and throw in free oil changes for the first year. It looks like we have a deal!"

As if on cue, the husband would grunt, still pissed off. The wife would say, "Honey, I want to drive home in a new car today, and that salesperson, Frankie, was so nice. He knows our son. And honey we've spent all this time here today, and they're going to give us free oil changes…"

And that's how their sales process worked. Universal Ford would simply wear people down. They'd make it so you either bought a car the day you walked onto their lot, or you'd NEVER go near that friggin' dealership again.

Either result was fine. They didn't care.

Frankie advised me that Universal Ford didn't believe in be-backs. (As in, "I like this car, but I'll be back") Frankie didn't believe in be-backs either. Along with a few other clever sayings passed on to me during my first day on the lot, Frankie told me, "Buyers are liars. Don't believe a thing they say to you."

I guess that was my first real lesson in sales…buyers are liars.

It was a heck of a first day in a sales career that would last forty years. I recall that there was something really exciting about the thrill of the chase. I wasn't quite sure if I liked the tactics being used but I remember thinking that selling things to people could actually be a *real job* for me.

THE INCREDIBLE LESSONS

When I look back at this sales process (then and now) it feels slimy. I assume it feels the same way to you. However, I've learned that if you're clever and aware, you can take lessons (nuggets) away from almost any experience, good, bad or slimy.

The lessons I gleaned from my first day on the lot were:

✓ **Don't be afraid to be ASSERTIVE:**

Frankie surely stepped in front of the other salesperson, which seemed unfair, but then again, the other guy **didn't stand up for himself**. It was interesting to watch. It made me think that, in most cases, it's easier to ask for forgiveness than ask for permission. But Frankie already knew that the other guy had no fight in him—hell, Frankie also knew the other guy wasn't a very good closer and blew most of his sales opportunities anyway.

It quickly became apparent to me that there was a *divide* amongst salespeople—haves and have-nots. (See The Pareto Principle, the *Law of the Vital Few*) I soon developed the hypothesis that if I was going to stay in sales, I'd have to make a choice of what side of the fence I'd spend my career on—a choice to become a HAVE, or have-not.

✓ **Always get them talking about their FAVORITE subject:**

As Frankie began moving the prospect through his sales process, he spent an inordinate amount of time getting them to talk about **themselves** and their family. This, of course, was their **favorite subject**. I saw the power of this on day one. I later learned that when you do this right, people LIKE you instantly, and they don't even know *why* they like you.

✓ **Successful organizations ALWAYS have a proven sales PROCESS:**

Of course, Universal Ford's sales process was horrible in many ways. I ultimately despised it because of its lack of honesty—but that's not the argument here. The point is that they actually HAD some sort of sales process—a track for salespeople to follow. We'd show them the advertised special and then we sell them OFF of it. Then we walk them into the showroom and pull up a car that fits the description of what they're really looking for. Then we put their butts in the car...etc.

Ultimately, if you have a process, even if it's flawed, it is always better than *not* having a sales track to run on at all.

Winging it will kill you in sales!

CHAPTER THREE

The Home of Low Prices

"Nobody…absolutely nobody, will buy from you unless they LIKE you."

—AL BOEGNER, general sales manager, Universal Ford

My first week on the lot at Universal Ford was a blur. My head was full of things to say, and NOT say—things to do, and NOT do. I did get four people *boxed* into a cubicle in the showroom during that first week. I even got my first two units sold. Serge seemed to be happy with my performance. He'd offered me some high-level motivational praise, "You're not bad kid. People seem to like you, yeah? You may make it around here."

Serge was no Tony Robbins.

It was Friday—the LAST Friday of the month. At that early juncture I didn't have much of a clue yet of how things really went down
at Universal Ford. It quickly became obvious that hitting a certain
monthly target of sold units was a big thing for the dealership. Frankie
told me that we could expect to be called into a sales meeting sometime
before our shift was over. Wow, I thought…an actual sales meeting! It
sounded so exciting to me. I imagined that we'd be called into a nice air-
conditioned room with tables and chairs. There'd be coffee and donuts
and other yummy snacks. I assumed that Al Boegner would discuss
sales forecasts and what the new models for 1979 were going to look
like. Then there would be some formal sales training. Surely Boegner
had to be some kind of genius salesperson and sales manager. I couldn't
wait for what he had to say. I was stoked for this meeting to say the least.

I had been on shift since 9:00 am. It was close to 4:00 pm and my
butt was dragging. Frankie and I grabbed a cup of coffee from the
catering truck that pulled up next to the body shop. We were kicked
back near the leasing office and I was wondering when this exciting
sales meeting would start. As if on cue, Serge's voice came on over
the loud speaker.

"Ladies and gents, Mr. Boegner would appreciate da pleasure of
your company in da back warehouse. Five minutes. Hustle back 'dere."

I inquired about the "back warehouse." Apparently there wouldn't
be a nice air-conditioned meeting room and no comfy chairs. Forget
about the snacks. The back warehouse was a huge corrugated steel
building. They used this structure to store the new cars that came in
off the truck. It was a gigantic metal frame with no windows and no
A.C., just a few roll up doors and some big fluorescent lights hanging
from the metal roof.

Like the walking dead, we all trudged to the back warehouse. If
you aggregated all of the sales and leasing people, there were about
sixty of us. Frankie told me that you wanted to stay close to the roll
up door because it would be the only place with ventilation, but as
soon as everyone got in, Serge slammed the door shut. There went

our ventilation. Serge, and two other managers, walked to the front of the room and stood quietly. There was a square windowless office in the corner. The door slowly opened and Mr. Boegner walked out.

Al Boegner was wearing the shiniest black suite I'd ever seen. He wasn't that tall, maybe five-foot-ten, but there was an aura of power about him. The room went completely silent as he walked to the center of the cavernous space. He stood in front of Serge and the two other managers. His eyes narrowed as his head moved slowly from left to right, scowling as he surveyed the crowd of salespeople. He didn't speak for about ten seconds, which seemed like an eternity. When he did open his mouth, what poured out was the most offensive tirade I've ever heard delivered to a group of professional salespeople. Even to this day, almost forty years later, it ranks number one in my distasteful speech category. Boegner placed both hands on his hips, unbuttoned his shiny, black suit coat, loosened his tie, leaned forward and let loose.

"You weak mother f_____s call yourselves salespeople? My f_____in' grandmother could move more units than you sorry bastards. We have three days to hit our number and if we don't make it I'll fire every f____in' one of you pieces of s__t."

Boegner's opening torrent almost knocked me off my feet. I glanced over at Frankie and the other veterans and none of them seemed fazed. They were deferential, but certainly not shaking in their boots. They'd seen Al Boegner's act before. I instantly realized that Boegner's distinctive communication style was probably standard operating procedure. Frankie looked at me and simply rolled his eyes. There was a handful of new guys like me in the crowd. Their nervous twitches were noticeable.

Boegner went on.

"You know what your problem is? You don't want to win bad enough. You mother f_____s are scared to death to make big money. You wouldn't know what to do with prosperity—a little more money in your pockets. How the f__k do you even go home to your family at night and look 'em in the face? I'll tell you what I want you to f____in' do. When a mooch walks onto this lot, you latch on to him like you're his long lost brother, sister, son, daughter or cousin. You stay on them like white on rice. If a swinging d___k walks on this lot you can bet he's here for one reason and one reason only. He's here to purchase a f____in' car. The question is, are you man or woman enough to sell him one? When they step foot on this lot, you reach out your hand, smile, and say, 'Welcome to Universal Ford, home of low prices.' Don't let them walk off this lot without buying a car. You become the son or daughter they never had, or their best f_____in' friend. You know why that's important? It's important because nobody... absolutely nobody, will buy from you unless they LIKE you."

Boegner was actually foaming at the mouth. He wiped the spit with his sleeve and then ended his motivational speech with a bang.

"Now get the f___k out there and sell some God d___n cars. It's my way or the highway, baby. Roll some units this weekend or hit the bricks you weak mother f_____s."

Boegner exited the steamy corrugated metal building, cutting right through the crowd. The assembly parted like the Red Sea for him as he led his three managers back towards the showroom and into his Fort Knox style office. The sixty of us, standing there, drenched in sweat, slowly began to disperse back to our posts. Thank God I only had another half hour on my shift, because I was in shock. Frankie and I walked back to the front line of the dealership. I asked him if Al Boegner was always that pissed off. He told me that Boegner was actually in a "pretty good mood" as things went.

As twisted and unconstructive as my first sales meeting was, I walked away that day thinking that one thing he said did make a lot of sense.

> ### "Nobody...absolutely nobody, will buy
> ### from you unless they LIKE you."

I thought about Frankie—that big smile of his—the way he was always trying to *connect* with people, asking them questions about themselves, getting them to engage with him. I never forgot what

Boegner said in the sweltering building that day. It made quite an impression on me. I worked hard to find a way to be likeable to prospects, peers and others ever since. It's funny what you can learn when you're open and hungry for any sort of mentorship you can get your hands on. My very first sales meeting, the one I so highly anticipated, was shocking, creepy and even a little demotivating. Maybe I subconsciously stored this experience as an early lesson in what NOT to do if I ever became a sales manager. The lyrics from Firefall's hit song that summer of '78, came to mind: *That's a strange way to tell me you love me.*

As unusual as my first few weeks on the car lot had been, it would get a hell of a lot more twisted.

THE INCREDIBLE LESSONS

It's weird, these events happened almost forty years ago and I can still clearly see Al Boegner's face, and recall and hear his words like it was yesterday. I believe that this is because the events were so otherworldly for an impression-able seventeen year old.

There's one sales related lesson I'd like you to take away from this chapter, and also one leadership/manage-ment lesson.

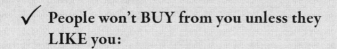 **People won't BUY from you unless they LIKE you:**

Wow. So simple. So TRUE.
You still have to do all of the OTHER things such as, engage, uncover needs, position your solutions and actually ask them to buy (CLOSE), but all things being equal, if they don't

like you, they won't buy from you. That was true in 1978, and it's even more correct today. Think about it...consumers have SO MANY choices in today's *flat* world, so many more than we had back then. In 1978 there was no Internet, hence less choices. More importantly, there was fewer ways to research all of the options and far less access to delivery. In today's consumer-centric society, if we don't like a brand, product or a salesperson, we're only one swipe away from MANY options.

Ever since I heard AL Boegner's words, my objective in a sales situation became to create a ***bond*** or connection as quickly as I could with a prospect. At first it was a smile, then I learned how to ask the right questions about them. My objective still today (when I'm in a position to ask somebody to do business with me) is to find commonalities with that person I'm talking with. I want to learn something about them so that I can truly ***connect*** with them in a personal way. My objective revolves around helping them become comfortable with me as a *thought partner* or trusted advisor.

And to think...this lesson was wrapped in a curse-laden tirade by a guy that had surely just done a few fat lines of blow. (Hey...it was 1978 in the San Fernando Valley!)

✓ **People will take action because of FEAR or LOVE...but** *love* **is always the stronger provocation:**

Motivation is a funny thing. I've written and spoken on this subject (as it applies to sales and leadership) many times. I have a whole proven premise on the word "motivation." I won't bore you with it. I'll simply give you the abbreviated version of my philosophy. To me, motivation is **not** an *external* job. Hence, we can't motivate anyone. The best we can hope to do is to **connect** with them and **inspire** them to identify their **internal** motivations (reasons) for doing the work. If they trust us and feel that we understand them and care for them, they will feel that **love** and search for all the reasons to do the work **with** us and *for* us. And sometimes, because they love working with you, they will do more for YOU than they would ordinarily do for themselves. We should never mistake the fact that ultimately, they will do the work for their **own reasons**, but when *love* is in play they're always inspired to do **more** and do the work **better**.

When Al Boegner brought all of us into that horrible metal shed and yelled at us, threatened us with termination if we didn't produce, it wasn't at all motivating to me. Not in the least. It didn't inspire me and it didn't make me like him. Did it provoke me to make sure I sold a few cars in the short-term so I could keep my shitty job? Sure. But I couldn't say that I felt positively motivated to go out and sell some cars due to his words and actions. In addition, the second or third time I had to stand there and listen to his pathetic rant, I just **tuned out**.

Did people FEAR Al Boegner? Some did, some didn't. Was that fear a catalyst for any increased production? Perhaps it was, but only on a short-term basis, and only for a few of the newer people. The reality of it was that anyone that was hard working and really talented left at his or her first opportunity. They went somewhere that they thought that they could be **loved**, or at least somewhat **appreciated**.

That's how salespeople tick.

Later in my career, I experienced *love* and *appreciation*. It was then that I learned and *felt* the difference.

CHAPTER FOUR

God Bless America

*"The quest for riches darkens the
sense of right and wrong."*

—ANTIPHANES, 4th century BC poet

I was several months into my illustrious sales career, and I'd moved enough Mustangs, Pintos, Thunderbirds and Fairmonts off the lot to validate that I actually had a *real job*. Buzz was happy, Serge was happy, and most importantly, I was satisfied with the decision I had made to sell *stuff* for a living. I was enjoying my early sales success, but something didn't feel completely right. I felt a measure of apprehension with regard to whom I was selling for, and *how* they were asking me to sell.

I didn't have a huge problem following the Universal Ford game plan, as long as the client was happy in the end. I got what they were doing. The advertised special was a loss leader. It lured people onto the lot. I was able to show the advertised car, but was always quickly able to redirect the prospect to the car they really wanted. All of my customers were pleased when they drove off the lot. I made sure of that. Unlike some sales reps at Universal Ford, I cared about people and wanted to see them get what they wanted.

My scripting was different than some others on that damn lot. It wasn't only the Catholic guilt, fear of Jesus and that Ten Commandments thingee that the nuns pounded into my brain; it was even more than that. I'm a Christian, but my beliefs were actually more personal than organized religion if that's possible; it was the voice and example of my parents in my head. I was raised to be kind and fair to people, to make sure that you went out of your way to help others. It was about my mom always doing things for others before she did anything for herself. It was the example of my father dropping everything and running to help a friend or neighbor whose car was broken down or water heater needed to be changed. I was taught that you help your friends and neighbors, not take advantage of them.

I just didn't have the DNA to screw people over.

It wasn't in me.

Since nobody in their right mind would buy the kind of vehicle they were offering as the advertised special, I never felt bad about steering them to a better-equipped vehicle that didn't look like a piece of crap on wheels.

On one particular Friday afternoon, the last Friday of the month, Serge and I were on the showroom floor talking. I took the opportunity to ask him what they did with those ugly cars they ordered for ad specials after they sat around for a week and didn't sell. I was curious because the ad cars always oddly disappeared after about five or six days. For example, we had a puke-green Mustang advertised a few weeks before. It was horrendous looking and (obviously) didn't sell. Then it was gone. Serge and I were standing next to a fully loaded red Mustang parked on the showroom floor when I posed that question to him. I'm not sure Serge really wanted to answer me, or really should have, but

I guess I caught him at a weak moment. He smiled his crooked little Canadian smile and pointed discreetly towards the red Mustang with his ballpoint pen, and then he walked silently into his office.

Nooooooo. It couldn't be!

The puke-green Mustang that we had on ad special two weeks before had black interior, no stereo, black wall tires and plain aluminum hubcaps. This was clearly a different car. This Mustang was red, with camel-tan interior; it had high performance tires, chrome wheels and the dash was loaded with every option the factory offered. I wanted to call Serge back over and tell him that he must be mistaken. Frankie had been standing there listening to the conversation. He waved for me to step outside and then he proceeded to give me a complete education on how he believed all Universal Ford advertised specials were "born again."

It seems the whole repugnant process was an open secret. The owner of the dealership apparently had a history with used car lots and body shops. His name was Emanuel Bugelli. Bugelli bought the dealership from the Bill Heath family in 1975. He changed the name to Universal Ford because of its proximity to Universal Studios. Prior to 1975, the place was a friendly neighborhood dealership that did business straight up with no gimmicks. But that all changed when Bugelli altered the selling method to a "turn over" (T.O.) system, the one where we weren't allowed to let a prospect walk off the lot until we turned them over to another salesperson. Bugelli didn't invent the T.O. system (Ralph Williams did...more on that later) but Mr. Bugelli took it to a whole new level.

I'm not sure how Frankie knew about the shenanigans and details that took place with the advertised specials, however he told me all about it "in confidence," of course. They had quite a slick program going on. After a week of using the stripped down vehicle as a loss leader, Boegner would order the lot boy to drive the car to the far end of the back warehouse. It sat there waiting for a similar trade-in to come onto the lot. The trade-in didn't have to be the exact same year, just the same model, and within a year or two of the ad special. For example, they parked the puke-green 1978 Mustang, and waited for a '77 or '78 Mustang to come back in on trade or repossession. They were basically the same models, as Ford hadn't made any major style changes to the body or interior packages. Because of the volume of units Universal Ford sold, it didn't take long for a similar model to arrive back into inventory.

So here's how the math worked. Universal Ford had paid the bare minimum for the new stripped down vehicle that was used as the advertised special. They would also pay the minimum value possible for a trade-in. So they had huge margin potential on each vehicle. They'd drive both cars to an offsite body shop and start playing Frankenstein. The nice tan seats were taken from the barely used trade. They were carefully refurbished to look like they were brand spanking new, and then they were dropped into the previous advertised car. A high-end stereo was installed in the dash of the former ad car, along with any other bells and whistles they could rape and pillage from the trade-in. The chrome wheels from the trade-in were removed, shined up and installed. Hardly used raised white letter performance tires were taken out of the body shop inventory and slapped onto the car. Finally, the car was sanded, primed and re-painted Ford racing red. The car was fully detailed and parked on the showroom floor. Finally, it was showcased as a new car that had been "dealer customized."

Oh...It was "customized" all right!"

I didn't ask Frankie too many questions that day. I didn't really want to know anymore than he'd already told me. What I did know was that, when they were done, they put a car out there for sale that was advertised as a *new* car, but it actually had pieces and parts on it that didn't come from the factory, and certainly were not brand new. The sticker price on the car would be thousands of dollars higher than what they paid the Ford Motor Company for the same unit— all PURE profit. Frankie told me that they repeated this process six or eight times per month. What they did with the used car trade-in was beyond what I could conceive, but Frankie thought that they were probably rolling back the odometers on those cars, and also adding back the missing parts from a source acquired from a "secondary" market, which was his code for stolen parts. I was never able to substantiate Frankie's information because anyone who knew the game wasn't exactly talking to a new guy like me.

After Frankie got done schooling me that afternoon, my head was spinning. I was still so naïve at that juncture that I actually asked him if the stuff Universal Ford was doing was "technically illegal."

Frankie laughed and said, "Shit, yeah, it is." Then he shrugged his shoulders and said, "But WE aren't doing anything illegal. We're moving the product they're paying us commission to sell. The liability is on them." Then he placed his hands over his ears, eyes and mouth. "Hear no evil, see no evil, and speak no evil. I'm just trying to make a living here, buddy...just trying to help my family make ends meet. They give me a nice check each week and I keep my f____n mouth shut."

From that moment on, nothing was the same. My small questions and concerns steadily became bigger questions and concerns. After that, I was never completely certain if the car I was selling someone was 100% factory new. I'm sure virtually all of them were, except for the Frankenstein Mustang ad specials, but still?

The voice of God came over the loud speaker and we were summoned to the back warehouse for the end of the month Boegner tongue-lashing. By this juncture, these sales meetings were simply amusing to me. A few of us regulars, including Frankie and another liner named, Steve Jackman, occupied our regular spot in the very back so we could do our best impersonations of Boegner without being noticed. Jackman did an awesome reproduction of Boegner. He'd hold his breath, get his face all red and then somehow get the veins in his neck to pop out just like Boegner's. It was an epic impersonation. We knew Boegner's script well, he'd tell us what pieces of crap we were for ten minutes, that we were all going to be *fired* and then we'd go finish our shift. However, on this Friday afternoon there'd be a twist to our end of the month meeting—a special guest would make an appearance. After Boegner got done with what I would rate as his *best* performance to date, a portly man with a dark gray pinstriped three-piece suit stepped forward out of the shadows. He was standing quietly behind the managers that stood behind Boegner. I didn't even notice him back there.

It was Emanuel Bugelli, the owner of the dealership. He NEVER came to the dealership—you never saw him. You just knew him by name. I swear, this dude was straight out of Central Casting. If Hollywood needed the perfect mob boss for their next Mafia themed feature movie—and Pacino and De Niro were busy—they should look no further. Mr. Bugelli had a Sam Giancana-like fedora on, and he was sporting a pair of Ray Bans. He slowly removed his sunglasses and placed them in his breast pocket. He took a handkerchief from another pocket and meticulously dabbed the sweat from his forehead.

I didn't know if he was going to bitch us out or have us rubbed out.

Mr. Bugelli cleared his throat, and in a very soft-spoken manner he began to speak about his parents moving from "the old country," and bringing him and his siblings along to America. He spoke eloquently, with a slight trace of a New York accent. He talked about his time spent on the East coast growing up—how hard his mother and father worked to keep food on the table during the depression. He recounted the family's move west to California, the land of opportunity. Then he began his dissertation on the "American dream."

"Home ownership was very important to my mother and father," he proclaimed. "When we bought our first family home it was a proud day for everyone. But to pay for that expensive home in California we all had to get back and forth to our jobs, and that requires owning a car. So while we think of owning a home as the American dream, that aspiration only becomes a reality if you own a motor vehicle first."

Bugelli went on to tell us that WE would be the Ford dealership that would "break all national sales records." He told us that WE would accomplish this by not only being the home of low prices, but we'd also be known as the dealership that "wouldn't turn anyone away for credit reasons." He even suggested we call everyone back that had been turned down for bad credit. During his short address to us that afternoon, Mr. Bugelli announced a new banking relationship with Security Pacific National Bank. He told us that nobody would be sent away without realizing their "American dream...a brand new Ford of their own in their driveway." He ended his brief talk by asking us to all join hands and sing God Bless America.

I swear!

And we did exactly that.

Everyone locked hands. We swayed from left to right and sang that damn song. It was bizarre, but also strangely moving.

Mr. Bugelli's little talk and song had fired up the crowd for sure, especially with the news that they could call back countless warm prospects in their Rolodex. These were people that hadn't initially cleared a credit check, but wanted to buy a car. They would coax those undesirables back onto the Universal Ford lot. We now had a bank that would supposedly loan *anyone* money to buy a new car.

We could now help everyone attain the American dream!

There was a stampede out of the warehouse. Salespeople raced to grab their dead files and locate an unused phone.

I had been on the lot since 1:00 pm and my shift was supposed to end at about 9:00 pm. It had been an odd day already, to say the least. But it would get just a little more odd.

THE INCREDIBLE LESSONS

There is only one lesson I think we can pull from this chapter, but it's a powerful one.

✓ **If something doesn't feel RIGHT, it probably ISN'T:**

I'm not going to suggest that every person, company or organization you work with will be perfect, but there's a big difference between *perfect* and a **lack of ethics, decorum and common decency**. In hindsight, Universal Ford certainly lacked all of those. I guess the old saying "where there's smoke there's fire" applies here. So while I don't want you to spend your time nitpicking the people and company you work with looking for *fires*, I would like you to notice it if you see the damn smoke!

From my ample experience, your **initial gut feel** of whom you're working with is almost always accurate. If the little man (or woman) inside of your head is telling you that something isn't quite right, then you should probably listen. **You can choose to ignore** something that seems wrong, simply because you're making good money. That's your choice. Just know that if you're working with people that do not operate with integrity, **it won't get better with time**. You are always better off to cut your losses, move on and upgrade your career.

Frankenstein Mustangs

CHAPTER FIVE

Mortal Sin

"God's eye does not slumber. He knows every sin that is hidden from the mortal eye."

—**ELLEN G. WHITE,** American writer

Miker" was in his late thirties. He'd been married and divorced three times and he'd sold cars at more than a dozen dealerships in the Valley. He was well traveled and well worn. His full name was William Michael Miker, but everyone simply called him "Miker." He was on our team, Serge's team. He smoked like a chimney, and he was constantly chewing sunflower seeds. He would spit them out all over the place, inside or outside, on your shoes, on his own shoes.

He was a chocolate mess.

One time he spit those damn seeds on Serge's office floor and I thought Serge was going to kill him. He wasn't allowed in his office

33

for a week after that. In addition to his other bad habits, he always seemed to have the faint odor of booze wafting off of his body. Frankie didn't much care for him, but Jackman and I liked him because he provided great comedy relief. In addition to his peculiar personal habits, he had a million awesome stories about the car business. It wasn't just the substance of his stories; it was the *way* he told them. He'd act them out, doing the different voices of each character.

He was very entertaining.

The sales department of the dealership officially closed at 10:00 pm, but if you didn't have a deal working, Serge would let you clock out at 9:00. Leaving at 9:00 that Friday night would give me enough time to get to the Red Onion before their cover charge kicked in, and that's exactly where I planned to go. It was 8:40 and I was watching the clock devotedly when Miker waived me over. He had an up, an older couple, and I could sense he was losing them—or maybe he *wanted* to lose them.

They were standing next to the advertised special. Our advertised car that weekend was a stripped down orange Ford Fiesta. It was hideous, but they had priced it so cheap that, of course, people were flocking in to see it. The couple looked to be in their mid forties. The husband was wearing a pair of well-worn blue jeans and a Pendleton shirt. He looked very blue collar, like he didn't have two cents to rub together, but he did have a checkbook in his hand. There seemed to be a discussion about *delivery* of the car. I heard the husband saying they were "all cash," and asking if they could "drive it home tonight," as I approached them.

Miker was in a cold sweat, looking like he couldn't cut and run fast enough. I'd only been in sales a few months, but I'd already begun to develop a sixth sense about sticky situations. I scanned the lot to see if there was anybody else around. If there was, I'd say, "Tag, you're it." Then I'd clock out, run like hell to my car and drive as fast as I could to the Red Onion. I didn't see a soul. The rule was, that if a team member asked you to take their up, you didn't have the option of turning it down. It took Miker about four seconds to make an excuse and disappear. So there I was, shaking their hands, welcoming them to Universal Ford, home of low prices. The husband was polite, but direct. He had the newspaper folded up under his left arm and that damn checkbook in his right hand.

"Son, let's cut through the small talk. We're here to buy this car, the one you advertised in the paper here". He pointed to the paper jammed under his armpit. "You're friend there, Bill or Mike, wasn't too helpful. Hopefully you can tell us what we need to do next, and if we have enough time to get the paperwork done tonight. We want to drive this car home. It's going to be a birthday gift for out eighteen-year-old son who just graduated from high school. He's a good kid, works two jobs and has had some health problems. We want to surprise him."

I was standing there in a daze.

The father talked about what they wanted to do for their son and the mother's eyes welled up. I was paralyzed—didn't know whether to crap my pants or go blind. I suggested they drive the car before they buy it. I was dancing—trying to buy time to find somebody on my team to flip these people to. The husband said they didn't need to drive the car. I asked them to take a careful look inside—to make sure the Fiesta had just the right equipment for their son. They said the equipment was "fine." I advised them that teenagers didn't like the color orange—it wasn't "cool." He told me that his son could have it re-painted later if he didn't like it.

I glanced at my Timex. It was 8:50. My opportunity to avoid a cover charge at the Red Onion was quickly slipping away. Selling another unit at full price before the month was over would be a good thing for my wallet, but dodging a cover charge and downing a cold beer was all I could think about. Based on the fact that this couple was dead set on buying the ad special, versus a regularly priced car, I had my work cut out for me. I looked around the lot again. It was a ghost town. There was nobody to turn these people over to and they were hell-bent on driving the orange Ford Fiesta home that night. I was trapped and I was exhausted. It had been an extraordinarily warped day. Learning about the crap that went on with the ad cars in the back, getting yelled at again by Boegner, joining hands and singing God Bless America with an old Italian guy in a pinstriped suit in a corrugated metal building—just weird.

I needed a cold beer, real, real, real bad!

All I could think to do was walk this couple into a box and go get Serge. Serge could fix this. I sat the nice couple down in an open office in the showroom. I told them I had a call waiting and my manager would help them with the rest of the transaction. They seemed happy with the delivery of this news.

I went to fetch Serge. His door was closed, but not completely. I knocked softly, but there was no answer, so I pushed it open and found him snoring in his chair. He had his feet up on his desk, no shoes on, an unlit Marlboro in his lips, and a half empty Molson Golden sitting in front of him. I woke him up and he listened to my explanation in a daze without saying anything. He slowly rose, put on his shoes and sport coat and tightened up his tie.

"Take me to dem," he snorted. "Introduce me, and den you wait in da showroom. I'll take care of dis and get dem hooked on another car."

I introduced Serge to them and closed the door to the box. I walked over and leaned up against the red Mustang, the one I learned was previously our puke-green advertised special. I waited for Serge to perform his magic. After what seemed like an eternity, the door opened. Serge had a check in his hand and a scowl on his face. He walked over to me and said, "You and Miker really f____d dis one up big time. I'm gonna' go take a leak, make them think I'm going to da Boegner's office, den I'll give 'dem one more shot."

Serge was back in the box with them for another ten minutes when I heard voices elevating—first Serge's, and then the husband's. I moved closer to the box and heard the husband say, "If you don't want to sell us this car, all you need to do is say so and then I'll go to the authorities."

Serge bolted out of the small office, slamming the door. He gave me a death stare, and then he took a deep breath and walked into Boegner's office. After no more than two minutes, the office door flew open and Boegner emerged with the couple's check in his hand. He had crumpled it up. He also gave me a look. It was a look I'd never seen before, or since—pure anger and disdain. I heard him mutter "dumb F___in' rookie," under his breath as he passed me.

In his eyes, I'd committed an inexcusable mortal sin.

I had all but SOLD the advertised special

Boegner and Serge entered the office with the nice couple. The door was closed for a moment, and then Serge came out and walked over to me. By now it was after 10:00. They'd have to pay me overtime if I stayed, so Serge told me to "clock out and go the f__k home." He tried to make me feel better by saying, "Kid, dis ain't completely your fault. Dese people are a little crazy, yeah?" He patted me on the back and I took off for a night of mindless partying that would now include a cover charge.

The way the schedule worked out, I had the next two days off—a rare real weekend. I was planning on going deep. I'd head over to the Red Onion, fake I.D. in hand, and I'd turn my brain off and get my weekend started. It was difficult to silence my head. I was interested to know how Boegner was going to talk that nice couple out of that orange Ford Fiesta, the car they wanted to buy so badly for their son. That car would be the boy's piece of the American dream and allow him to drive to his two jobs, but would Boegner even sell the car to the nice couple?

I was more than curious about how it would all go down after they sent me home.

I'd have to wait a few days to find out.

CHAPTER SIX

Bait & Switch

"Nobody's all good or bad—nobody's all light or dark. Every human being has different aspects and facets to them. And there can be something noble and something really dark and dangerous going on in a person at the same time."

—ANNA GUNN, actress

By the time I hit the lot on Monday afternoon, the story was all over the dealership. They were all laughing at how Miker and I "couldn't steer a mooch off the advertised special." Miker wouldn't come anywhere near me, and Frankie just smiled and shook his head when he saw me that afternoon. My other close friend on the lot, Jackman, told me a little bit about what he'd heard, he said it got ugly and he suggested I get the full story from Serge.

I went into Serge's office. He closed the door and told me exactly what happened. Al Boegner couldn't get them to budge off the car. After trying every trick in the book, Boegner began to insult them. Serge said it was "brutal" to watch. The wife started to cry and wanted to leave, but the husband wouldn't back down. He stood his ground. He kept demanding that they take his check and sell him the car, or he would "go to the authorities." It was then that Boegner reared back and hocked a spitball that went all over the contract and the check. Serge said that the husband stared straight ahead into Boegner's eyes. When that disgusting move didn't shake the husband, Boegner reared back and spit in his face. Serge said that the green package landed right on the man's forehead. Then he told me that Boegner yelled, "get the f__k out of my dealership you cheap mother f___er!"

I had never seen Serge crack, but while he was telling me the story of what happened to that nice couple, his voice waivered and he became emotional—remorseful. He referred to Boegner as a, "f___in' deranged animal." Serge told me that the husband calmly took out his handkerchief, wiped his forehead, grabbed his wife by the hand and left.

I didn't sell any cars that day.

When I saw someone walk up or drive up to the lot, I turned and walked the opposite direction. It was the longest eight hours of my life.

* * *

Weeks had passed since Boegner's spit in the face incident. My production had steadily declined. I was going through the motions—phoning it in.

My relationship with Frankie had also begun to change. He wasn't as friendly and open as he'd been before. He wasn't cold, just quieter and a bit distant. He was in training for a closer's position, so he was in the box with prospects more, and out on the lot much less. I chalked up his detachment to that—the pressure of training for a promotion. I had also begun to take notice of extracurricular activity in the general manager's office and also in the finance office. The dealership was suddenly receiving a much heavier flow of guests, and most of them wore dark suits and red ties. My buddy, Jackman, told me that the "suits" were bankers from Security Pacific. The men with the nice suits came and went, large rolling briefcases full of files in tow.

It was late on a Thursday afternoon when Frankie approached me. He asked me if I wanted to grab a bite after our shift at our local joint, Sitton's NoHo Diner. I had some tentative plans later that evening and wanted to get home and kick back for a while, so I declined. He kept asking me to join him, like he had something he wanted to talk about, so I unenthusiastically agreed.

Our shift ended and we rendezvoused at the diner. We sat down and ordered. Frankie didn't immediately open up. He sat there, doodling on a napkin with his ballpoint pen, so I finally broke the ice. "What's going on, Frankie? You don't seem like yourself lately, dude." He didn't answer immediately. Then he fired a question back at me.

"You happy at Universal Ford?"

My answer was quick and sarcastic.

"I'd be happier if I was playing golf and drinking beer every day, but my father requires me to have a job since I'm not in college and still living at home. At least at this job I don't have to do manual labor, so..."

He cut me off and shifted into telling me that I was a "good salesperson" and I'd learned a lot and could probably "move up to a better dealership or position somewhere." I told him that I considered Universal Ford a stepping-stone, but I'd only been there a few months and I wasn't ready to cut and run yet because I didn't have a better option. He went on again telling me about how I could do better. I listened to him patiently and then asked, "You trying to get rid of me for some reason, Frankie? I don't get it. If Universal Ford sucks so bad, why are you staying here and promoting up?"

He didn't answer, he just took a bite of his patty melt. After extended silence he got to the root of what he wanted to tell me.

"Listen Joe, you can't share this with anyone. I'm only gonna' tell a few people that I like. The dealership is under investigation. The bank is breathing down their necks and the DMV is crawling around in their files and up their asses. The federal authorities have also recently taken an interest...there's a lot of shit going on."

I picked at my French fries—tried to process his words.

It quickly became clear to me that his little rap on how I could "do better" if I "moved on" was his way of warning me that some heavy crap would be coming down. However, that still didn't explain why he was staying there and bucking for a promotion.

"So, as a friend, you're telling me to hit the bricks because all this stuff is going to go down, but at the same time you're training for a promotion? I don't get it, man."

Frankie finished his sandwich with two big bites, leaned back in the red vinyl booth and unloaded the rest of the information he was harboring inside.

"Look, this place is doing so much illegal shit that it's hard to list it all. Let me give you the Cliff Notes. Universal Ford sells partially used cars to people and tells them that they're new. They take used cars in on trade and roll back the odometers so they can charge more for them based on the Blue Book value. They violate existing state laws by using bait and switch advertising techniques. They can't refuse to sell an advertised special to a customer, in fact, they're *supposed* to sell those cars and then post the report of sale on the showroom floor window. This dealership also alters new car window stickers and has even changed VIN numbers on units."

By this point I'd stopped eating—was simply listening to his tirade, and he had a lot more to tell me.

"My protected sources tell me that the dealership may have recently started slightly altering the credit reports and loan applications of customers. When we were told that we could sell ANYONE a car, regardless of their credit, it wasn't because our bank suddenly softened their loan requirements. It was because Bugelli and Boegner decided to fudge loan applications after customers signed them. When all of this shit comes down, a few people may be going to jail."

I'd begun to digest what Frankie was telling me. But all of this stuff didn't explain why he was STILL there. In fact, in light of all that he apparently knew from his "sources" why the hell wasn't he running for the hills, just like he was advising me to do? I pressed him again on that point and he finally dropped the best little nugget of them all.

"A local T.V. station is doing some investigative journalist thing. It all started with your nice couple, the ones Boegner spit at. They phoned the consumer advocate at the local CBS station. I've been talking to a reporter from Channel Two for a few weeks. Sometime soon I'm going to be wearing a hidden camera and microphone. They have several assistant producers that are going to pose as customers—they're gonna' come in and ask to see the advertised special. These undercover producers are going to try to buy the advertised car and then all hell is gonna' break lose. They're going to lure one of the closers, and hopefully Al Boegner, into the box and get the whole thing on hidden video tape."

Frankie was getting more and more elevated—his face was getting red as he continued his garbage dump of inside information.

"I agreed to do all this because I hate these mother f____s. Especially Boegner. Serge has been recommending me for promotion for months and that asshole Boegner didn't want to promote me. He must hate Mexicans or some shit. f___k him! He's going down if I have anything to do with it. I told them everything I knew. The federal authorities won't touch me, and they'll probably only slap most of the closers and salespeople on the wrist. They want ownership and executives—heavy fines and possible jail time. But you don't want to be around when the undercover CBS producers come in and all of this gets aired on the eleven o' clock news. You certainly don't want to be employed here when the authorities show up. You don't want to have them suspend your sales license. That will probably happen the same day that the State and Federal authorities come in with handcuffs for ownership. "

I picked up the tab at Sitton's Diner that day.

That was the least I could do.

*   *   *

I was standing in the showroom at Crown Oldsmobile in Pasadena, next to a brand new 1979 Cutlass when the segment was aired. The local CBS affiliate didn't wait for the eleven o' clock news. They broke the explosive story on their five o' clock edition and then aired even more footage at eleven.

Frankie's advice had not fallen on deaf ears that day at Sitton's Diner. I ran for the hills.

It had taken several months for the bank, the DMV and the federal authorities to collect and sort out all the evidence. They had gathered a TON of damning proof, hard copy, video and audio included. The T.V. producers showed up impersonating a couple that was interested in buying the advertised special. I recognized Frankie's voice in one of the taped segments, but they blurred his face. Al Boegner was priceless on camera—a real star! He called the undercover producer and his make-believe wife every name under the sun and dropped enough F-bombs that the bleeping sound was almost continuous at one stretch.

They padlocked the doors of Universal Ford.

The DMV officials detained the salespeople, took their basic information, confiscated their California Automobile Sales Licenses and sent them home. Serge and three other closers were questioned, but I learned later that none of them were charged with anything.

As the story goes, the T.V. station producers may have collaborated with Security Pacific Bank executives to devise a clever way to get Mr. Bugelli to come to the dealership. The bank president demanded a meeting with him or something—I'm not certain—threatening to pull their financing deal. Hence, Bugelli was there to do the perp walk along with Boegner.

So perfect!

Oh, and there was possibly a *silent* owner that nobody knew about—really silent. The "Bald Eagle" Ralph Williams, was reportedly somehow connected to the Universal Ford operation.

Mr. Williams was the notorious and legendary car dealer that had already suffered some scrutiny from the California authorities. You can still go on YouTube today and search videos of when several of his employees flipped out—they go nuts and call him a "bald son of a bitch." They bust him out and call him a *crook* right on live television. Search the 1968 Bayshore Chrysler Plymouth commercial...it's a classic! His own employees feel compelled to tell the buying public just how crooked he was.

And the same guy, Ralph Williams, taught the ownership of Universal Ford everything he knew!

Supposedly, by 1978, Williams was unable to formally own a dealership in California, but apparently that didn't stop him from cutting some sort of under the table deal with Bugelli. When the dust settled, Universal Ford was shut down for forty-one counts of illegal conduct and sales tactics. This included bank fraud, falsified DMV documentation and various illicit sales maneuvers. Ownership was barred from operating car dealerships in California for a long period of time and there were massive fines. There was no jail time however, as Bugelli and the rest had the best lawyers money could buy.

As previously mentioned, I watched this entire saga unfold live on the five o' clock news from the comfort of my private desk on the floor of Crown Oldsmobile in Pasadena. Crown Olds was a well-respected dealership and it was a pleasure to work there. Most importantly, it was there that I started learning how to do things right—sell things the *right* way. I was eighteen, had only been in sales for nine months, but had seen and learned so much already.

My *real* life in sales had just begun.

THE INCREDIBLE LESSONS

I guess that there are two (maybe less than obvious) lessons from this chapter and the whole Universal Ford experience that I'd like to point out to you.

✓ **You can LEARN from anybody: (Or any situation)**

Like the quote at the beginning of this chapter states, "Nobody's all good or bad," except for maybe Al Boegner. LOL! Think about it...as screwed up as Boegner and the Universal Ford thing seemed (and it was a twisted experience) I still walked away having learned a great deal. I learned from Serge, I learned from Boegner, I learned from watching everyone and everything going on around me, good, bad and ugly. When you stop to think about it, if you're in a somewhat challenging or negative situation and you don't choose to **take something of value away** from it, then it is really a shame, and also a gross waste of your time.

✓ **PEER mentorship is invaluable:**

Along with the very smart concept of taking something positive away from a bad scenario, there is another HUGE lesson I want you to think about. Having peer mentors can be critical for your **survival** and **growth**. Frankie was my first peer mentor. He was instrumental in helping me feel comfortable from day one. He was there to make observations and to also tell me things that my hierarchy couldn't or wouldn't tell me.

If you are not searching out peer mentors you are missing a big key to surviving and thriving in today's professional landscape. I think peer mentorship and peer advisory is more important now than ever before, simply because business and life tends to be **more complicated**. The complication comes from **more available choices and options**. This creates the need to make many **more decisions** on a daily or weekly basis, small and large. If you are **making all of those decisions in a bubble**, especially the big ones, without sounding boards, good luck!

CHAPTER SEVEN

Blind Ambition

"Things don't just happen in this world of arising and passing away. We don't live in some kind of crazy, accidental universe."

—SHARON SALZBERG, author

S elling cars at Crown Oldsmobile was completely unlike my prior experience at Universal Ford. None of our salespeople were out roaming the lot and sidewalks because we weren't allowed to aggressively approach prospects. We sat at our own neatly arranged desks on the showroom floor. We politely took our turns with the people that walked in—everyone was so well mannered. We didn't turn people over to other salespeople. We closed our own deals and we tried to give everyone a fair shake.

It was so terribly unexciting.

I hated it.

I'm only half serious when I say that. The short experience at Crown Olds did offer me a new perspective—one that suggested that there was a right and a wrong way to sell things. My sales manager at Crown Olds, Dominick, was a soft-spoken person who deeply cared for people. That didn't make him a pushover; in fact he had a great killer instinct for closing a deal. He wanted to close every person that came into the dealership; he simply believed that it had to be done with integrity. He would put his arm around my shoulder, walk me out to the lunch truck and throw some wisdom down, such as, "Joe, you know you've done it right when a person buys something from you and it's their idea, and they feel that they're in control of the process."

Dominick taught me to ask a lot of questions of each prospect. He taught me to listen carefully and to catch things most salespeople would miss. His method wasn't to focus on product or price; his philosophy was to position the right car as the right solution based on the needs of the prospect. He believed in educating prospects, building great value into the conversation.

I don't recall exactly why I left Crown Olds, but I'm fairly sure it had to do with the boredom. I was also experiencing a level of frustration. The interaction with prospects was awesome and closing someone was a huge high, but the waiting around for people to walk in was killing me. I had a short attention span anyway, and boy did I go bat-shit crazy as the minutes and hours ticked away between selling opportunities.

The perfect excuse for an exit from Crown Olds came along. My Uncle Mike was going back to the homeland (Italy), and wanted me to travel with him, so I gave my notice. The trip to Italy would take most of the month of May and upon my return I spent most of June playing golf and drinking beer. One evening, near the end of June, Buzz showed up in my room as a Blue Oyster Cult album was spinning on my turntable. He asked me to follow him into the kitchen.

When I got there I spotted the Daily News. It was opened to the Classified's section and there was that damn red felt tip pen.

I'd been down this road before.

If I had proven anything, it was that I could make some interesting career decisions by throwing darts at the newspaper. I was about to try my luck at career Russian roulette again, but this time, I thought, "I'm really going to nail it!" Instead of calling ads that were just marked "Sales," I narrowed the search down to, "Outside Sales."

The advertisement that wound up catching my attention was:

"I need three people to call on my current accounts"
Contact Bud Cole

The classified ad was blinder than Stevie Wonder, but that didn't stop me from calling it. Two days later I was driving to my interview wearing my dark brown suit. The office was on the second floor of a nondescript three-story building adjacent to the runway at Van Nuys airport. The sign on the door read, "Trans Pacific." The receptionist led me into a large private office. There were two gigantic, ornate desks, one on each side of the office. There were two men standing in the middle talking. The taller man let me know that he'd be with me in a moment. I glanced at the nameplate on each desk. The one closest to me said, "Bud Cole." That desk was messy, like a small tornado had just touched down on it. The other nameplate read, "Norbert J. Cieslak." That desk was spotless—hardly anything on it and nothing out of place. I observed the two of them carefully as they finished their conversation. They were discussing second quarter sales results. I sized them up. It wasn't hard to guess who belonged to which desk.

Bud Cole was about six foot-nine inches of untidiness. His unique look began with a really bad rug—a toupee so obvious and mismatched to his coconut that NASA could probably identify it from space. His distinctive style continued with a pair of granny glasses that hung from his neck by a small gold chain. They were the kind your grandmother would wear. He had no suit coat on and his rumpled shirt featured one rolled up sleeve and a tail that didn't completely make it into his pants. His trousers were a smidge too long, buckling over a pair of brown shoes and frayed at the cuffs as he dragged them around. Bud Cole would never be mistaken for a Brooks Brothers model.

Conversely, the guy I assumed was Norbert Cieslak was a study of corporate splendor. He didn't have a hair out of place and he wore a black suite that was perfectly tailored. The cuffs of his crisp white shirt were monogrammed with the initials, "NJC," and his black loafers were so shiny that the reflection of light blinded you when it hit them just right.

Because these two shared an office I assumed they were managing partners in whatever the enterprise was, but they couldn't have been more different—a real life incarnation of The Odd Couple. It wasn't only their desks and manner of dress; it was also about the way they communicated. Bud, the guy with the bad rug flailed his hands as he spoke. He was loud, and I noticed that there was spit in the corners of his mouth that sometimes went airborne. The other guy, Norb, spoke softly and eloquently; arms crossed and one hand rubbing his chin like he was Albert Einstein, solving the mysteries of time and space.

As the odd couple finished their conversation I recall thinking, "Please God, let it be Norb that interviews me." As they wrapped up, Norb approached, introduced himself and told me I'd be, "In good hands with Bud."

Bud Cole introduced himself.

I'm not a tall man—maybe five foot eight on a good day, so Bud hovered over me like Bigfoot as he pumped my hand. My eyes immediately locked onto his rug. It was fascinating to me. His real hair—which there wasn't much of—was clumped around each ear and it was salt and pepper gray. His toupee was a dark brown color. His furry coconut animal didn't only stand out because of the poor dye match; it was also conspicuous because it was crooked. I remember thinking; did this guy even check out a mirror when the toupee salesman sold him the rug? Or, did he take one look and say, "Damn I look good! Nobody's ever gonna' know I'm mostly bald if I buy this toupee!'"

My fascination with Bud's man-made hair gave way to his dissertation about the history of the Trans Pacific agency, a division of Pennsylvania Life, or, "Penn Corp," for short. He and Norb had partnered to build one of the most profitable sales divisions in the United States for the parent company. Bud and Norb held Agency Vice President titles.

He went on to explain how he and Norb had created an accident insurance product for the company. It was designed for small business owners and self employed people. It created a safety net for them and in many cases could save their home or business. He told me that they had, "Thousands of current customer accounts," that needed to be called on and that most of these current policyholders would buy new coverage at renewal time. He described their sales training program as, "The best in the industry." Bud talked about the chance for rapid advancement into management, and then he said the thing that I wanted to hear.

"There's NO CEILING on what you could earn here. Your income isn't limited. We have an open geography and territory. You can sell anywhere to anyone...make as much money as you want. Many of our solid salespeople earn over $80,000 a year and the top producers earn over six figures." This was 1979, so $80,000 in 1979 would represent well over $250,000 in 2018 dollars!

But I'm not sure I heard anything after he said, "$80,000."

I recall that we shook hands and Bud said something like, "You're hired." Then he waltzed me out of his office and introduced me to a nice lady named, Joyce. Joyce gave me some forms to fill out and told me I needed to be "In her class," the following Monday. I didn't exactly know what the class was, and wasn't sure how the compensation plan worked, but I was reluctant to ask questions because I didn't want Bud to change his mind and not hire me.

When I got home, I sat down at the kitchen table and my mother, Helen, and I looked over copies of what I had signed. She asked about the base salary and I couldn't tell her what it was. We dug a little further and saw that I had signed an independent contractor agreement and an application for an insurance license. I recall telling my mom that I think I'd accidentally agreed to a job selling accident insurance door to door, completely on commission.

My mother turned to me and said, "Nothing happens by accident." It took me years to understand what she meant...and how right that statement was.

The last thing I thought I'd be doing while my friends were off at college drinking beer, chasing girls, and earning their degrees was selling insurance, door to door, on commission. But at that juncture, all I could think to focus on was that $80,000 a year that Bud Cole told me I could earn.

If I could ever earn that amount of income, it would be TWICE what my father—or anyone else in my family—had ever earned.

THE INCREDIBLE LESSONS

This is more of a strong opinion than it is a lesson, however I'm going to ring it up under the lesson category because this truth has come back to roost so many times in my professional and personal life that it makes my head spin.

✓ **Nothing happens ACCIDENTALLY**

Of course, I had no way of knowing it at the time, but circling that stupid blind ad in the paper and signing up to get an insurance license—stumbling into selling those stupid accident policies door to door—was **NO accident**. The training I received at Penn Life (and having that insurance license in my hot hands) eventually became **my ticket to earning millions** of dollars in commission and bonuses. It was my entrée to creating **financial freedom**. I now know that God and the Universe were involved when I answered that blind ad in the paper, there were too many signs revealed to me over time to believe otherwise.

It is hard to see things as providential, especially when negative stuff happens in your life—stuff that isn't so cool, but I assure you that every single experience, negative or otherwise in my career, became a **connecting bridge** to the **next thing**, and the next. Of course, I have the luxury of almost forty years of experience as an entrepreneur to reflect back upon. I have the advantage of **a long arc of time** to see that nothing was an accident; the events were all there to **teach me something** I'd use later and to **prepare me for something great.**

The arc of time is a beautiful thing. It can teach us so much. But only if we're taking notice.

CHAPTER EIGHT

Basic Training

"Excellence is an art won by training and habituation. We are what we repeatedly do. Excellence then, is not an act but a habit."

—ARISTOTLE

PennCorp Financial was a conglomerate of smaller entities built onto the skeleton of the ancient Pennsylvania Life Insurance Company. PennCorp's home office was close by in Santa Monica, but oh so far away from the Trans Pacific division's sleepy outpost near the Van Nuys Airport, way out in the Valley. The president of PennCorp, Stanley Beyer, was recognized as a wunderkind in the industry. He had become consummate at the art of building shareholder value. Beyer had methodically turned the sleepy old-line life insurance company into an accident insurance cash-generating machine.

Beyer drove sales growth by borrowing a few proven principles from the legendary W. Clement Stone. He ripped off and duplicated Stone's model almost verbatim. Because of PennCorp's success, Beyer had pocketed humongous performance bonuses and he'd begun conspicuously consuming. By 1979 he was living in Bugsy Siegel's old mansion in Beverly Hills, right next door to Burt Bacharach. He wasn't bashful about letting everyone know that he'd just commissioned the famed architect, John Lautner (Frank Lloyd Wright's protégé), to build a ten thousand square foot mansion on a promontory point in the swankiest part of Malibu—The Colony. That home would later be valued at over twenty million dollars.

Apparently, there was a lot of moola in the little accident insurance policies that Trans Pacific and the other subsidiaries were selling on the street. Trans Pacific was a star cash cow for the parent company. The rent for the nondescript office adjacent to the Van Nuys Airport was cheap, and annual production was increasing by double-digits each year. Anything Bud and Norb did to keep the premium dollars flowing was fine by Stanley Beyer. As the story went, both Bud and Norb were once part of the home office executive-level team in Santa Monica, but both had been exiled for different reasons. Bud had been banished because of his caustic nature—he had no filter—he was not PC. Norb had been deported for the opposite reason, he was too PC. Norb had no opinion—nothing to add to the conversation. He was perceived as of little value.

The product that transformed Trans Pacific into such a profitable division was called, "Safe Drivers." The Safe Drivers policy was a $39.00 instant issue accident plan that covered the policyholder whenever they were in a car, bus or truck, anywhere in the world, any time of day. The policy paid the claimant cash if they were in an accident. There was a schedule of benefits including a small monthly income if they couldn't work. The field force of Trans Pacific would canvass the business parks all day long, offering the low cost, high benefit plan, door to door, to business owners and their key employees. When the five o' clock bell rang, the agents shifted their prospecting from business parks to residential neighborhoods, looking for any sign of a self-employed person. Any work truck with a phone number painted on the side was our excuse to walk up to the door and start knocking.

We were making Stanley Beyer and the shareholders of PennCorp wealthy beyond belief, $39.00 at a time.

After I came home from my interview with Bud and reached the realization that I'd applied for a license to sell insurance and would need to pass a state exam, I cracked the books and began to study. If I told you that I wasn't a very good student that would be an understatement. My study and test taking skills were horrible. It was not my thing. I failed the state insurance test twice, but squeaked by on my third attempt. The third try was my last chance as far as Bud Cole and Trans Pacific were concerned. When I walked into the Trans Pacific office waving the hard copy license in the air there were multiple sighs of relief.

Trans Pacific was my first outside sales position and also my first commission only experience. Things would be a little different than the car business. In that previous gig, I had a base salary. It wasn't much, but if you had a bad month, you could still steal a paycheck and pay the rent. The other big difference was that in the car business, people came to you. Even if you stood in one place with your feet glued to the ground, eventually somebody would cross your path and ask, "Hey, can you sell me this car?"

Outside B2B sales didn't work that way. You could show up at the office each morning, but nobody was going to hand you a paycheck. They may hand you a cup of coffee and a jelly donut, but not a paycheck. You had to actually put down the donut, get in your car and go find some people to talk to. A transformation would have to take place in my head. I'd need to form new habits and that would require a great deal of discipline. Simply put, I'd have to drag my sorry ass out into the field every day if I wanted to make a living.

But before I'd get the chance to make my first field call, there was basic training.

The training room at Trans Pacific was the meeting room and the break room all in one. Bud told to be there at 8:30 a.m. sharp. I snuck into the back of the small room at 8:28, took off my suit coat and draped it over a folding chair. Grabbing a maple bar, I did a quick head count—fourteen people including me. There didn't seem to be a certain type of person that Trans Pacific hired. Out of the thirteen other people sitting in that training room, I couldn't discern that there was a prevailing particular pattern of race, color, creed or gender. Later that day, one of the few young dudes in class—a guy I made friends with named, Larry Story, blurted out, "Eighteen to eighty, blind crippled or crazy. It looks like they'll hire anyone around here." I couldn't disagree with my new friend's acerbic statement. There was a guy in the front row that must have been seventy-five or eighty years old. He walked with a cane and had two humongous hearing aids sticking out of his ears. Those hearing devices looked like damn 747s.

Our trainer entered the room from an adjacent side door at exactly 8:30 a.m. He walked to the middle of the room, glanced at his clipboard and used his index finger to silently click off and count the bodies. When he was satisfied, he walked to the back door.

He closed it and locked it.

"Good morning ladies and gentlemen. My name is William Darnell and I'm going to be your instructor for basic product and sales training. You are to be here on time every day this week. The door will be locked at 8:31 a.m. each morning. We will take a lunch break from noon until 12:59 p.m. and then we'll resume class at 1:00 p.m. sharp. You'll be excused at 5:00 p.m. each day. Please don't ask to be excused earlier than that."

He circled the room looking each one of us over as if he was a drill sergeant inspecting his new batch of buck privates. After he surveyed us he removed his rather thick horn-rimmed glasses and wiped them off methodically, posing to look us over again. I would later learn that Darnell was retired military and had reached the rank of sergeant in the Marines. He wasn't a tall man, perhaps five foot nine, but he was fit and muscular. There wasn't anything warm and fuzzy about him. His presence said, "I'm here for business...and I hope you are too."

Monday—day one—was spent learning about our company history and our flagship product, Safe Drivers. We were all handed a voided out policy and asked to follow along as Darnell read it word for word. After lunch, he chose several people randomly to come up to the board and list as many of the limitations and exclusions of the policy as they could recall. I faired pretty well at that pop quiz but some others didn't. After a short afternoon break we were all handed a five-page script. It was the boilerplate sales presentation for the Safe Drivers product.

Sergeant Darnell told us, in no uncertain terms, that we would not be allowed to represent Trans Pacific in the field until we had, "Memorized the company presentation word for word." I looked at Larry and we both looked down at the five-page script, shuffling through the stapled, purple-inked mimeographed pages. I quickly estimated that there were several thousand words to the script including common prospect objections and all of the required rebuttals to those objections. Larry meekly raised his hand and asked, "Mr. Darnell, do you mean that you want us to *learn* the script—ya know, be able to get through most of it—be able to use this as a guide when we're out there pitching?"

Darnell snatched off his glasses. He glared at Larry and asked, "Is that what I just said, son?"

Larry, now sweating, answered, "Well, that's why I'm asking, cause you said, 'word for word' and there's lots of WORDS here in this presentation and the objections and rebuttals, and I just figured you meant we need to get the gist of it and be able to get through it..."

Darnell cut Larry off and launched on us.

"Look, your job this week—during basic training—is to memorize this presentation word for word. Your only job is to know this damn script backward and forward by the time we break camp on Friday evening. I didn't say that you could just get through it or learn the gist of it. You'll learn this presentation word for word—be able to give a presentation without missing a beat and then offer a scripted rebuttal to each of the most common objections we've listed. Do this and you can begin selling Trans Pacific products in the field. If you don't learn this script word for word, then you'll be back in my class next week...and the week after that if necessary. Any more questions?"

You could have heard a pin drop.

The old guy in the first row was squinting up at Darnell with a glazed expression on his face, like he'd just been addressed in a foreign language.

"Okay, now pair up and start working on the memorization. Role-play a little. Start with the introduction and the first three paragraphs. Chop, chop...we still have fifty minutes left on the clock today."

* * *

It was the most intense week I'd ever spent in a classroom. It was the first time I could ever remember actually giving a crap about what I was studying.

It was Friday, just after lunch. There were only eight people left in our class. Six people had already quit—they just walked away, before they ever got started. Larry and I had our own little wager on who was going to make it through the week and who wasn't. By Friday I was $3 in the positive on our pony race. I nailed the first three quitters. One of the guys was forty-something—a real big mouth braggart who had sold everything under the sun in his illustrious career. I bet Larry that he'd wash out quickly. The second quitter was a woman, probably in her thirties, who questioned everything. "Why do we say that? Wouldn't it be better if we said this?" Larry and I couldn't wait till she raised her hand to interrupt Darnell with a stupid-ass question. It was awesome to watch the sergeant get so ticked off. His face turned red and the veins in his neck popped out.

She bailed on day three.

I had also picked the old man with the two humongous hearing aids to drop out, but come Friday he was in the front row, ready to give his presentation. I had to applaud that, but watching the shrinking down of our class was a great lesson to me in and of itself. It signaled to me that the commission sales game was a vastly different endeavor than a W2 position with a base salary. The people sitting in the seats on day five truly wanted to be there. We'd made a definite decision to do the work and to win. Observing our basic training week helped me understand that a commission only sales force was truly a volunteer army.

Larry and I had also made a pact to nail it. We decided to do some role-playing together after class. He was twenty-two and I had a fake I.D. so each afternoon after class we slinked over to the airport bar and sat there repeating the words over and over again.

Hi, are you the owner or manager of the business? Great. Can I ask you a funny question? Are you a safe driver? Do you have a pretty good driving record? Great. Then I think this will interest you too. We've already written it for most of the business owners in the area. I'll show it to you. Now for $39 they don't promise you the moon, but they do offer you four very important benefits...

After four nights at the airport bar, many Coors Banquet Beers and even a few shots of Cuervo Gold, we could recite the presentation and all of the rebuttals, word for word, in a coma. When we showed up on Friday we were locked and loaded. We would be graduating out of basic training that Friday afternoon. The acid test for graduation was delivering a flawless presentation to sergeant Darnell and overcoming at least two of his objections. Bud Cole would step into the training room to watch the final exam. Larry and I nailed it. After I completed my presentation, Darnell took off his glasses, put his arm around my shoulder and told the class, "That's what this presentation is supposed to sound like." I caught a glimpse of Bud Cole in the back of the room. He was leaning up against the back corner with a little smile on his face. He winked at me, nodding his head in approval.

By the end of the day, six of us would be moving on, including the old guy, which surprised the crap out of Larry and me. The two people that didn't make it were crushed. One younger girl, just out of college, kept getting flustered and began crying during one of the role-plays. The other person that failed was this really sweet guy named Jatinder. He struggled a bit with the English language.

The week of basic training taught me one very important thing— something that proved to be essential to my philosophies as a sales trainer later in my career. Darnell demanded that we memorize that darn script word for word before we got out of his class. He knew we'd change words or tweak a phrase once we gained experience and found our voice. But he and the company wanted to make certain we had a proven track to run on as we got started. They knew that if we memorized the presentation and used it, we would have some measurable results. After that, we would then begin to internalize it—understand the psychology of it and as we grew more comfortable we would personalize the presentation—make it our own.

Trans Pacific knew that if they were haphazard with their training, allowing people to slide with a sloppy presentation that was a little off track, they could become WAY off track in a hurry. This would occur as a new salesperson stumbled. They'd lose confidence and then begin to experiment in their isolated bubble. When I later became a field trainer I always asked a person to learn their front talk and presentation word for word first—have some success with it, before they began experimenting.

Larry and I, of course, celebrated over a few beers during happy hour over at the airport bar. We even got a few of the others to join us. We were all stoked to start field training. Darnell had told us that we'd be assigned to a sales team and manager on Monday.

Monday couldn't come soon enough for me.

THE INCREDIBLE LESSONS

Basic training in July of 1979 was awesome for me—the best week ever. I took three very cool things away from the experience.

✓ **There's a big difference between just showing up, and actually COMMITTING to do the work:**

We began the week with 14 bodies in the room. Only 6 graduated. **To me it's about COMMITMENT**. Either you ARE committed to doing the necessary work or you are NOT. Maybe some of the others in that training class had better options. I didn't. I made up my mind on the first day that I would do what was necessary to learn and/or memorize whatever they handed me. With me, **it all starts with making a definite DECISION to WIN** at something. Then after my decision is made, I'll locate all of the **resources** I will need to get that thing done. I'll figure it out somehow, but it's already a fait accompli—ultimate success is a **done deal** in my mind before I get started.

✓ **You can't PICK 'em:**

The old guy with the huge hearing aids...I wouldn't have picked him in a million years to graduate, but he did. The really smart college girl...I wouldn't have thought she would fail, but she crashed and burned. That week showed me that **I couldn't predict who would make it in sales** and who wouldn't at first glance. This was a valuable lesson to me as I began to recruit and select salespeople later in my career. The reason that you can't pick 'em up front is that you can't see their heart—**you never know what's in a person's heart** until it is revealed.

✓ **WORD TEXT (a track to run on) provides amazing CONFIDENCE:**

I had so much **confidence** after **memorizing** that script and graduating that I thought I could step out into the field and close people at will. As you will soon read, it didn't work that way, but I did begin my outside sales career with the confidence of knowing **what to say** to them up front, how to educate them on our product and how to handle (rebut), an objection. I had **a basic track to run on**. I felt competent enough to have a conversation. That competence gave me confidence.

In today's world, where we have a tendency to present differently—**engage versus giving a pitch**—you may think that *memorizing* word text is not the right thing to do. On the contrary, those that **memorize, internalize** and **personalize** the right questions, and learn *how* to ask those killer questions in the right way, close at a much higher percentage than their peers and competitors who are winging it.

I will also tell you that we have FAR LESS TIME **to get our point across** than we did a decade or two ago. This demands that we become **razor sharp** with what we want to say or ask. It is more critical than ever to have great and **clean word text**.

CHAPTER NINE

Down The Street

"There's no lotion or potion that will make sales easier for you, unless your potion is hard work."

—JEFFREY GITOMER, author, sales trainer

"This is the sharp young kid I told you about, Tommy Trojan."

Bud Cole liked to assign people nicknames. The handle he gave Tom Smith was too convenient. Tom was a USC man. Bud was a UCLA graduate. Tom was in his late forties, tall, a great California suntan, and he possessed matinee idol good looks. His perfectly styled salt and pepper lid, piercing blue eyes and genuine smile made you feel like he could sell air conditioners to Eskimos.

"Joe Buzzello, right?" Tom shouted from across the crowded and noisy break room. "I heard you knocked it out of the park in Darnell's training class. We're going to spend the day in the field together—have some fun. Grab some coffee, we're going to start the sales meeting."

Bud and Norb worked their way to the front of the room and Bud screamed at the top of his lungs and called the meeting to order. He and the other sales managers began a cheer, or a chant. I wasn't sure what the hell it was. Everyone stood up and followed Bud's lead.

"To be enthusiastic, you must act enthusiastic. To be enthusiastic, you must act enthusiastic. To be enthusiastic, you must act enthusiastic. OH BOY...am I enthusiastic!"

Bud bellowed out the words as spit flew from his mouth onto the old guy from basic training class—the one with the huge hearing aids. He was in the front row again.

I stood in the very back.

When the cheer was finished, the room erupted in crazy loud applause and random whoops. Norb stood there with a stupid grin on his face, letting Bud run the meeting. It was standing room only. The next twenty minutes was filled with recognition—sales results from the previous week. Each of the sales managers that reported to Bud and Norb took turns stepping forward and bragging on their team. After they were done, Bud did a countdown of the top five producers for the week. He had their names written on cardboard strips that were slid into position on a wooden leader board on the front wall. He called out their income for the week—big numbers— bigger than I'd ever dreamed of earning. The meeting ended with another cheer or chant, I'm still not quite sure what to call it, even forty years later.

Although the chant felt awkward, it did wake me up and make me smile. Even though I wasn't the guy getting the recognition that morning, I felt a certain rush when the sales figures were read. Between the chant and the recognition of top producers I left the room with a lot more energy than I came into it with.

Before I had time to grab another donut, Tom and I were piling into his Chevy Malibu and heading down the 210 freeway towards the San Gabriel Valley. Tom smoked his Salem cigarettes like they were going out of style. He only cracked his window an inch. I figure he wanted to soak up as much of the poisonous carcinogens as possible. He asked me about myself, then went into a long dissertation about the work we were going to do that day.

He had a stack of what he referred to as, "customer tickets." He explained that these were people that had purchased the $39.00 Safe Drivers plan a year prior, and it was their renewal time. We were going to visit them and, "service their accounts," he advised me. Our first call was on a pallet-manufacturing yard in Baldwin Park. Tom identified and approached the business owner, a crusty old white guy who didn't recall buying the coverage in the first place. The business owner didn't look much like a business owner to me. He had an ancient pair of blue jean overalls on that looked like they hadn't been washed since color TV was invented. He smelled interesting— a combination of sawdust, motor oil and body odor.

I sized him up immediately as a *waste of time.*

"What the hell is he going to buy?" I thought.

Tom had a big smile on his face and apparently no worries in the world as he showed the old guy the renewal ticket with his name on it. Tom said, "I'm from the home office in Santa Monica and the reason they sent me out here today was to make sure you know about all of the benefits you already have and to make you aware of some very important changes they've made to your policy."

The second part of Tom's opening line got the owner's attention. The business owner took off his cap, scratched his head and said, "Well okay, if they sent you all the way out here from Santa Monica I guess I can give you a minute, but they better not have raised my premium. Come into my office."

As Tom followed the policyholder into the office, he turned and winked at me.

What I saw over the next thirty minutes was magic.

Tom asked him if he had his original policy handy. Tom showed him what the big white catalog-sized envelope would look like, pointing to the picture of the home office. It seemed to jog the owner's memory. The old guy walked over to an old, rusty, beat up file cabinet muttering, "Yeah, I remember buying this. What happened to the guy that sold it to me?" Tom told him that the agent had moved to another area. (I'm 100% sure the agent quit!) Not breaking stride, Tom grabbed the envelope, opened it up, surveyed the policy and then took out a yellow pad. Tom outlined the benefits the owner already had—sold him on the original plan all over again—and then showed him the, "additional benefits" he'd been "approved for." By the time Tom was done the owner was writing out a check for $240.00, which included the accident riders Tom drew out on the yellow pad and had added to the original plan. Oh, and Tom also sold him a Safe Drivers Policy for his wife.

As we left, the business owner shook Tom's hand, thanking him profusely for coming all the way out there to see him. We were in and out in under thirty minutes and Tom had bumped the premium from $39.00 a year to $240.00. When we got to the car I asked Tom how much commission he'd just earned. He smiled and advised, "We get fifty percent of the additional premium sold, so roughly $100." But then, while he lit up a fresh Salem, Tom added this little nugget, "You never count your money when you're sittin' at the table, Joe."

Apparently Tom Smith was a Kenny Rogers fan, a philosopher and an expert salesperson.

Our break was short.

We sat in the car silently for a few moments as Tom made some notes and put the riders he'd just written into his folio. He finished his smoke, tossed it out the crack in the window and warned, "Don't get too comfortable, we have some cold calls to make down this street."

I was going to see the presentation I'd just spent a week of my life memorizing put into action by a real pro.

THE INCREDIBLE LESSONS

There are three lessons from this chapter that I want to cull out for you.

✓ **We all need to see proof of concept:**

The cheer (or whatever the f- it was) actually got my juices flowing. It was just stupid enough to wake up the crowd. But the **recognition** of top producers...hearing their names called—seeing those big commission income numbers go up on the board—that was awesome! I couldn't wait to get out of that office and into the field to start pitching. Seeing the real commission dollars being earned told me one thing—**It COULD be done**. Somebody was doing it.

I needed that proof of concept.

We ALL need that.

✓ **It's expensive to make assumptions about prospects:**

That old guy—the business owner that dressed and smelled weird—I made an instant assumption that he wasn't going to buy anything from Tom. Hell, I wouldn't have made a bet that he was going to renew his $39.00 existing coverage. **Tom didn't make any such assumptions**. Tom was experienced enough to know that you don't GUESS at who's going to buy and who will not. Tom simply went about his business—**he stuck to his sales PROCESS**—until he either made a sale, or had a compelling reason to blow the taco stand.

It's **expensive to GUESS** and also very foolish. Pros don't do that. They don't let their mind play *tricks* on them. They allow for their sales process to **uncover** the **truths.**

✓ **Don't stop to celebrate:**

After Tom made a big sale, he didn't stop. **He didn't pump his brakes** and slow his own **momentum.** He knew that the best time to work *(and get through the numbers so you can get to another YES)* is when you've just scored. Weak and lazy salespeople stop to celebrate after a win. They lose whatever **momentum** they had. They go cold. Strong sales pros might take a minute to smile and feel the rush, but that's about all.

Then they **hit the gas** again.

July of 1979—Tom Smith (left) and an acne-faced eighteen year old trying to figure out how to make a living selling those $39.00 accident policies.

CHAPTER TEN

Breaking The Seal

My first week in the field with Tom was incredible.

He was a pro's pro.

Tom alternated his efforts between calling on the stack of existing customer tickets that he had stashed away in his briefcase, and strolling down the street, cold calling. When I tell you that he appeared to be, "strolling" down the street, that's exactly what it looked like to me. It seemed so effortless. He even whistled while he went from door to door, I kid you not. I didn't make any approaches or presentations that first day. I simply observed.

On day two I got my chance to finally try out what I'd learned in basic training. In the car on the way out to El Monte, Tom let me know that I would be making an approach or two. I was up to bat after lunch. Tom checked my sight seller to make sure it was in strict compliance with company guidelines and then he pointed over at a strip of businesses on Ramona Boulevard.

"Why don't you go down the street right here and make a few walk-ins, Joe, you ready?"

When he asked me if I was ready, my pulse rate immediately soared. I took a deep breath, trying to calm myself as we strode toward the first door, but my heart beat even faster as we got closer to the business. I knew that damn approach and presentation word for word—could recite it in my sleep—but that was classroom stuff—this was real. I was about to ask an owner of a business to listen to an eighteen year old kid who was still wet behind the ears. I felt a burning sensation in my loins, like I had to pee, as I walked into the door. I approached the man standing at the counter of the tire shop. He barked at me, "What can I do for you, son?"

I'm pretty sure I wet myself a little. Absolutely nothing came out of my mouth.

I'd frozen up!

He repeated his request, "How can I help you, son?" Something very damn incoherent tumbled out of my mouth, but I don't recall what those words were, and they weren't at all what I'd learned in class. I'm not sure it was English. When the business owner cut me off and growled, "Not interested," I thanked him, turned, and rushed out the door. After we walked out to the curb, and Tom stopped laughing, he put his arm around me and told me that this kind of thing happened a lot and he said that it was pretty funny to watch. He even got me to laugh at myself. "Come on," he snorted, "You know the damn pitch. Bud said you killed it in class. Just focus on the script, ask the question, 'Are you a safe driver?' Once you get going you'll be fine. The words will roll right out of your mouth. Pretend you are in front of Sergeant Darnell. Nobody's scarier than that sum' bitch."

He was still chuckling at me as we walked into the small automotive repair shop and it was in that shop that I gave my first full sales presentation.

It was glorious and I was awesome.

Not!

However, I was able to get through it and I rebutted two objections. The business owner didn't buy, but I walked out of that place with the biggest smile on my face. Tom slapped me on the back and told me my pitch was, "rock solid." I made another half dozen or so walk-ins that day, and a few more on day three. I came close to closing a deal on several occasions but fell short. I was still a little robotic with the pitch and Tom suggested I not worry so much about getting every word right. He also suggested I make more eye contact.

I had a tendency to look down at the sight seller.

On day four I was ready to put the pen to the paper. In the car, on the way out to West Covina, I told Tom that I was ready to close somebody. We called on several customer tickets in the morning, stopped for lunch and he picked a couple of streets out of his Thomas Guide for us to do some cold calling.

Oh, and for you Millennials that don't know what a "Thomas Guide" is, it was a prehistoric form of GPS. The Thomas Guide was an 8 x 6 spiral bound two-inch thick map of every street in a particular city or area. So if you wanted to find an address back in 1979, you would go to the trunk of your Chevy Malibu, take the appropriate Thomas Guide out of the giant stack of Thomas Guides you kept in a cardboard box, and then strained to remember what page Baldwin Park was located on. You'd then flip to page 39 (because that's where most of Baldwin Park was located) and you'd let your fingers do the walking.

Tom selected Azusa Avenue in West Covina for me. This street had a mixture of retail shops and small light industrial business parks. After about eight or ten walk-ins we found a business owner in a Mexican Bakery. He stood still long enough to let me pitch him. It was right there amongst the cake batter and powdered sugar that Joe B. wrote his very first insurance policy. The hair on my arms stood straight up as I walked out the door, real fast—so the guy wouldn't change his mind and ask for his check back. I still had the $39.00

check glued to my right hand as Tom and I high fived. I had only earned $19.50 in commissions, but it felt like a million bucks.

This business is going to be easy, I thought.

THE INCREDIBLE LESSONS

This is a short chapter, but I want to point to three lessons that can be critical for new salespeople to ponder.

✓ **Real sales professionals make the job look EFFORTLESS:**

When I tell you that Tom appeared to be "strolling" down the street with not a care in the world, whistling while he went from door to door, it was 100% accurate. Tom wasn't focused on any individual result. He really didn't care if the next person he approached said, "yes," or "no," or they said, "get the hell out of here!" He simply didn't care. Tom was a **PRO**. He wasn't focused on any **singular** response. He was focused on a **body of work**—a larger cluster of data, namely, sixty walk-ins.

Tom approached selling with great inquisitiveness. He was always **curious** about how his day would go. **He never forced things.** He'd say things like, "Let's see if we can **get our numbers in** today. Who knows what will happen." He'd tell me, "Let's not get too hung up on any one response. Let's put all of the *pressure* on the numbers and *relax*."

✓ **There's a DIFFERENCE between the classroom and the field:**

I had 'aced' the classroom portion of my training. I was confident with my knowledge of the scripts, but when I had to pitch to a real live prospect, I almost pooped my pants! LOL! Make sure that you understand that the classroom and the *real world* are **different**. Understand that if you miss a word, phrase, or question, it's no big deal. It's not like your prospect even knows that you missed something.

When I mumbled and stumbled, Tom simply suggested I get **back on script**. That's why I'd **MEMORIZED** and **INTERNALIZED** the content of the presentation. I was now in a position to *deliver* it and begin to **PERSONALIZE** how I delivered the message. Because I had taken the time to memorize and internalize my word text I had a **reliable track to fall back on** until I became comfortable with the adlib.

✓ **If you can't LAUGH at yourself…you're toast:**

This is a fairly direct lesson. If you take yourself (and what you're selling), **too seriously**, you are **setting yourself up for failure**. You're probably not saving lives on a daily basis. Oh, I know…what you do is important and your products make people's lives better, I get it. But **nobody is going to DIE** if you don't get the appointment or close the deal.

Don't place that extreme level of importance on each micro-opportunity and what you do for a living in general. **Be easy on yourself.** Learn to **LAUGH** at yourself. If you can't make fun of your own weaknesses and human fragility (and your prospect's stupidity in some cases), you won't last in sales!

CHAPTER ELEVEN

Spaghetti Logic

"Quitting is the easiest thing to do."
—ROBERT KIYOSAKI, author, *Rich Dad, Poor Dad*

The euphoria of my first sale and my inaugural week in the field with Tom carried me through my first solo week, but it was different being out there all alone. It was as if I was learning to walk a tightrope. Week one provided a comfy safety net named Tom Smith. Week two did not. There was no safety net, no Tom Smith.

There was nobody there to have lunch with.

There was nobody there to get me laughing when someone kicked me out.

There was nobody there to tell me to keep working the numbers after a horrible ZERO for something streak of cold calls.

It was just ME out there.

It was very damn lonely and I felt isolated.

The other thing that was pissing me off was that there were no existing customer tickets to call on.

Tom explained to me how the game worked on day five. He told me that the customer tickets were considered "golden" and you didn't get any of them until you proved that you could "swing the kit down the street" and open up a reasonable volume of new accounts. It was like I was stuck inside the movie, *Glengarry Glen Ross*, and he was delivering the famous Alec Baldwin speech. So the customer tickets would come my way once I proved myself cold calling, and cold calling was what the hell I was doing—all day...every day.

Like everything else with Trans Pacific and PennCorp, they had a very definite system for cold calling. They handed me a stack of small cards. The cards were entitled, Countdown to Success. The cards had five columns for the five workdays and the numbers 1 – 60 printed vertically down each of those columns. You were supposed to cross out each number when you walked in the door and made an approach. You were to circle the numeral if a decision maker allowed you to give a presentation and then place a number of units next to the circle if you actually sold something.

Of course, the objective was to hit the wonderful number of sixty walk-ins each day. Tom drilled it into me that, for some magical reason, a reason he couldn't even explain, sixty walk-ins/attempts was an *enchanted* number in our business. His rant went something like this:

"Joe, I can't tell you why this works, but if you cross out sixty walk-ins on your Countdown to Success card each day, the sales gods will reward you. If you don't, then they'll punish you. I've had days when I wrote a lot of business during the first half of the day, so I slacked off during the afternoon and took it easy. So, on the next day or two...well...it was as if the universe was saying to me, 'It's time for you to pay the price.' Then I've had days where I made the sixty walk-ins and I couldn't close anyone to save my life, but the next day...everyone said, YES.

The numbers just work and you have to trust them...you can never cheat them."

So, Tom had this whole rap about the sacred numbers and he all but guaranteed me that if I walked into sixty doors a day over a five-day period of time (and I stayed on script), then I'd make a good living and could expect the following predictable results:

- 12 – 15 business owners would stop and listen to my pitch
- 3 – 5 would say "yes" and allow me to write them up
- That would equate to about $100–$150 of commission per day

Now this was 1979. While $150 may not sound like a lot of money to you, you have to realize that $150 a day way back then is equivalent to approximately $500 in today's income. I could definitely make a good living selling the stupid $39.00 Safe Drivers policy, but that was only going to happen if I actually did the work, made the cold calls, did the walk-ins—sixty times a day—five days a week.

The only question would be...was I willing to commit to that block of work?

As week three and four dragged on, I realized that I was hitting a wall. It was partially the loneliness—feeling *isolated* in my daily activities. I believe it was also the inability to process rejection and failure appropriately and place those two common reactions and emotions in their proper context—but I was wilting on the vine. I was even starting to feel like I'd made a big mistake getting into B2B commission sales.

It was Friday afternoon, late summer, 1979.

I pulled out of the field early.

I had just completed a rather lackluster week. I'd made a few sales but experienced too many crushing defeats for my delicate, eighteen year old psyche. As the massive rejection piled up on top of me like wet, heavy sand, call reluctance set in. The reason I went home early that day was that I simply couldn't get out of my car and walk into another business. I was paralyzed by my feelings. My emotional gas tank was empty. I started to think some very negative and self-destructive thoughts. My self-talk sounded like, "guys like Tom Smith can do this because people like him are *born* salesmen. They rolled out of the womb with a silver tongue. I'm an eighteen-year-old uneducated nobody. What business owner is going to listen to me?"

I was tripping big-time, spiraling downward and I didn't want to talk to Tom about it. I was avoiding him. I didn't want to let him or Bud down and I was embarrassed about my stupid emotions and my inadequate results. Buzz cruised into the driveway at 5:30 pm that Friday evening and we all took our places around the dinner table. I dished myself some of mom's spaghetti, and then Buzz asked me how my week had gone.

That was a question I anticipated he'd ask.

I wasn't looking forward to answering it.

As human nature would have us do, I began to justify all of the various reasons for my lack of success to date in my new career. Of course, I began to suggest that the products, the territory and even my manager were the roots of my problems. My dad was one smart cookie for a guy who didn't have the advantage of any sort of formal education. He was a great listener and extremely level headed. Buzz was cooler than the other side of the pillow. He just puffed away on his Camel, ate some spaghetti and took it all in. I was honest with him about some things; I told him that I'd pulled out of the field early. I remember the conversation in vivid detail.

Like it was yesterday.

"I think I'm gonna' go in on Monday and quit," I told him. "I don't think this thing works, and I'm not sure I'm cut out for commission sales."

My dad leaned back in his chair. I could tell by the look on his face that he wasn't thrilled with my decision.

"Okay, Sport. You can do anything you want. It's your career; it's your life. Quit if you want," he told me. "But, I'll tell ya...I've never quit anything just because I was failing at it, especially if I saw others around me doing well. If you want to quit, you should go out and have a solid week first, figure some things out, then tell them you're quitting. That way you'll be leaving for the right reasons—because you don't like the work—not because you're *failing* at the work. You can leave with your head held high, a winner."

My father was an engineer. He was pragmatic and logical. It was hard for me to argue with the logic he was dishing out, but I was a teenager, so I had to try.

"Dad, yeah, I hear what you're sayin', but this sales thing is hard. It's mostly cold calling, and I'm getting beat up out there. I'm not sure their process even works."

He nodded his head like he understood, and that he was in agreement with me, but I could tell he wasn't going to let me off the hook.

"You got home at what time today, Sport?" he asked.

"About 2:30 p.m.," I reluctantly answered.

'Well, that doesn't sound like a full day's work," he sniffed. "How many cold calls did they tell you to make each day—how many doors do they want you to walk into?"

"Sixty," I told him.

"How many did you walk into today and this week?" he asked unemotionally.

I reached into my pocket and pulled out the small Countdown to Success card. It was still damp from sweat.

Glancing at the card, I noted there wasn't one day during the current week that I'd walked into more than twenty doors...and my efforts decreased as the long week wore on. There were a couple of circles each day and even a few sales. But when you were selling those $39.00 accident policies, you had to have more than a *few* circles and sales to make a living. On that day—Friday—I'd put out the puniest effort of the week. I'd only crossed off eight doors before getting back in my car and heading home with my tail firmly tucked between my legs.

"I walked into eight doors today," I finally admitted.

He leaned back and rubbed his chin. I wasn't sure if he was getting ticked off and planning to unload on me, or if he was going to abide by my decision to quit commission sales. He was quiet for a moment; then he spoke.

"I can't tell you what to do, Joe. Again, your job, your life. But, ya know what I'd do if I was you? I'd go out next week and walk into the sixty doors a day, just like they told you to do. I'd repeat that effort for the entire week, again, just like they taught you. I'd personally place their system, and their numbers, on trial. What's the worst that can happen...a few people kick you out? Win, lose, or draw, if you have done all that—exactly what they asked you to do, and you still don't like the work by the end of next week, you can quit. But the difference will be that you'll walk away knowing you gave it your all—100%. You can leave with your head held high, knowing you didn't fail to do the work. Does that make sense, Sport?"

His suggestion made too much sense.

After that, Buzz went back to paying attention to spaghetti on his plate. He didn't say anything else. The conversation was over.

The ball was in my court.

The reason Buzz's sage advice made so much sense to me then (and still holds up today), is that he was simply challenging me to set my emotions aside, put in a full week and put the pressure on the system—the numbers. I decided to follow his advice. I went out that next week with a VERY different attitude. I had only one clear objective, which was to cross out all sixty numbers on their stupid Countdown to Success card each day so that I could prove it didn't work. I was obsessed with reaching that goal of walking into sixty doors each day. Without realizing it, I was putting the pressure on the system.

I was getting out of my own way.

By the close of business on Tuesday of the following week, I'd already sold twelve units of business—my best week ever...and it was only Tuesday. I'd begun to realize that if I walked into sixty doors each day, I didn't have to be a great salesperson or closer. Because I was focused on putting pressure on the numbers, the rejection didn't seem to have a negative emotional effect on me. I had short-circuited my faulty wiring—removed negative emotions and fears from the equation. Buzz had challenged me to get out of my own way, and by doing so I'd stumbled onto one of the key concepts and attitudes that I would teach for the next forty years. I *reframed* rejection into nothing more than a metric result on the road to a YES, rather than a crushing emotional defeat or failure.

I walked into a minimum of sixty doors each day that week. On Thursday evening, I stayed out until 7:45 p.m. trying to find the six-tieth person to approach. By the end of my week I had an awesome block of production and had earned $550.00 in commissions!

I must tell you that Tom Smith was right...there was something magical about walking into sixty doors a day. I'm not sure I can explain it either, but that enchanted number of sixty just seemed to remove *luck* from the equation. That's an important factor, because if you sell things on commission for a living, you sure as hell don't want your livelihood to depend on "luck."

I was flying high on Friday afternoon and barely made it home in time for mom's dinner that night. My parents knew I was having a good week. I didn't have to tell them. My dad saw my energy and the smile on my face. The conversation that night with Buzz was short... and very sweet.

"So, I guess this was your last week," he stated somewhat sarcasti-cally. "You gonna' tell 'em you quit on Monday?"

He asked me that question knowing what my answer would be. I just smiled.

"Thanks for talking me off the cliff last week, dad. Thanks for challenging me. I think I got the hang of this thing."

I did have the hang of it.

I'd learned a valuable lesson, a lesson that was spurred on by my father's challenge and my sense of personal pride. I learned how to get out of my own way and let the numbers work for me.

So there you have it; my father furnished me with the greatest lesson I've ever learned in sales, and he'd never been in sales. His *spaghetti logic* stuck to me like wet pasta to a hot pot.

My father wasn't a salesperson or a business owner, but he did know a thing or two about surviving. He certainly knew how to pull himself up by his bootstraps so he could win in life. His father died when he was eleven years old. His beloved mother suffered a nervous breakdown under the financial stress of trying to raise him and his two siblings. He was effectively orphaned at a rather young age.

Buzz didn't earn his high school diploma; he had to work two jobs to support himself. When World War II broke out, he enlisted and went off to Europe to serve his country. He became a master mechanic while in the service. Upon his return, he learned a few technical skills at a trade school in Philadelphia. He eventually became a watchmaker and a precision mechanic. After relocating to Southern California in 1954, he became an entry-level aerospace engineer at North American Rockwell. He was an integral part of the turbine engine balance test crew of engineers that put a man on the moon. Think about that for a minute.

Orphaned at a young age.

No formal education or money.

He became an aerospace engineer

He helped put a man on the moon!

With all of the odds stacked against him, my father was able to get out of his own way.

I lost my father to lung cancer in 1987. He saw some of my early success, and I know he's seen the rest of it from where he sits right now. Buzz was an inspiration to me and still is. I hear his voice in my head everyday. I've been blessed to have a lot of great people like him and Tom Smith play a hand in my career along the way. I always tell people, I'm lucky; lucky I wasn't lazy, and also lucky that I could take direction and accept mentorship.

Fortunately, at a critical juncture early in my sales career, Buzz offered me a way of thinking during one of my mom's spaghetti dinners.

Let's just call it a little bit of *spaghetti logic.*

THE INCREDIBLE LESSONS

So many lessons to pull out of this chapter...micro and macro, so let's get started.

✓ **You have to learn to work in ISOLATED conditions:**

After the *safe* week with Tom, I had to go **SOLO.** I had to learn how to work on my own, in *isolated* conditions. Most of the time, in commission sales, you're going to be **alone** with your thoughts. You're going to have to learn how to **control your self-talk** and *coach* yourself. You must develop tools in the way of **mindsets** and **philosophies** that you can pull out and rely on when things aren't tiptop. Several chapters in the book, <u>The CAP Equation</u> can greatly help you form these vital mindsets.

✓ **Every sales process/sector/industry/market has MAGIC numbers:**

When Tom initially mentioned the **magic** of walking into sixty doors a day, it was just him talking—jabbering away. He was very precise in telling me that I couldn't (ever, ever) *cheat* the numbers and expect to win, but I didn't really hear

him. It took me going out into the field and experimenting with **different volumes of prospect outreach** to fully
understand what he was trying to tell me. It was when I put
their recommended numbers to the test that I realized **the
magic number thing always worked**. I didn't become a con-
sistent top producer until I became completely committed
to putting the pressure on the numbers and the system.

Bottom line...you have to learn what your magic numbers
are and then you have to *honor* those numbers.

You can never *cheat* them!

✓ **You have to be able to PROCESS rejection and
    failure appropriately:**

I learned early in my sales career that the emotions of
feeling *rejected* and feeling like you *failed* have to be carefully controlled. We have a tendency to put **labels** on things.
When you are new in sales it's easy to say, "Hey there's a lot
of *rejection* out there." Okay...sure, I get it, but tell me, are
they rejecting you personally? How could they logically be
doing that? In most cases, they don't even know you. Hence,
personal rejection doesn't really exist. Are they *rejecting*
your product or company? Maybe. But think about it, if
they don't meet with you face to face, or they meet with you
and don't completely take the time to *understand* your offer-
ings, are they really even properly rejecting anything?

Nope!

So that solves the word (and feeling of), **rejection**.

How about "failure"? Does *failure* exist? I will offer you a
mindset on this. First, the only time that you actually and logically **FAIL** in sales is when you make **a conscious decision**

to walk away—quit. Then...I will agree. In that case, you have certainly failed. However, in any scenario short of that, any and all results are simply data **clusters of feedback**. Any **result**, yes, no or maybe, is simply **input** that is there to **inform you** on what your work is returning on investment (ROI) and how you may be able to improve the ROI. In other words, you can use this **valuable feedback** to determine:

- How your **message** is being received in your core marketplace
- To what degree your **products** are effectively solving problems
- What **volume of outreach** is necessary to meet your income goals
- What **changes** or tweaks you should make to your market strategy

Now if you don't carefully *analyze* **your results** on a weekly basis, and you choose to mindlessly work without *listening* to the feedback and input, God bless you, and good luck. On the other hand, if you use that **valuable feedback** to **improve your conversion ratios**, then there is no result that you can logically categorize as a **failure**.

In fact, a NO is merely moving you closer to a YES.

So, logically, **"failure" doesn't exist** unless you quit and walk away.

✓ **Get out of your OWN way (emotionally) and COMMIT to the work:**

My dad's words were incredibly powerful to me. They were then, and they are now. What I learned about sales—and about myself—from suffering through those first few agonizing weeks in the field with Trans Pacific are lessons that have lasted a **lifetime**. One of the things that became clear to me that week and the following months, was that sometimes **the gap** between where you are and where you want to be could seem insurmountable. Oftentimes, it feels like you must be the only person feeling that way. The truth is that **you aren't the only person that ever felt like quitting**—giving up and walking away. Most top sales producers, leaders and successful entrepreneurs have faced similar gaps.

What my father so wisely pointed out to me was that **there is a difference between winners and losers**, and the way they think, feel and respond. The key difference is that winners figure out how to **close their gaps**. Losers often stall out and/or **quit** before they figure things out. I also learned that these gaps that seem so large are most often very small issues that can be overcome with a small **shift in attitude** or a little work on a **key competency**.

The other thing that I learned from that specific conversation with my father is that, YES, **there are "winners" and "losers" in life**. I apologize to those of you that may be offended by those labels. (No I don't!) Those of you that believe these words are somehow damaging to our self-image (and that everyone should receive a participation trophy just for showing up), probably shouldn't be reading my work. LOL! Life (and especially business), doesn't work that way. My father understood that. **He knew that life wasn't fair**, whatever the heck "fair" means. He knew that **simply showing up doesn't get the job done**.

The difference between winners and losers was clear to my father, and hopefully it's clear to you also.

CHAPTER TWELVE

Read and Grow Rich

"A capacity, and taste, for reading gives access to whatever has already been discovered by others."

—ABRAHAM LINCOLN

Bud Cole liked to stalk people.

He'd get bored sitting in his big, stupid office staring at Norb's empty-headed smile and he'd make his way into the meeting room. He'd target someone and then circle them—like a Mako shark. I watched Bud corner Larry Story one day and bark at him for twenty minutes straight, mostly about the length of his hair.

Out of the corner of my eye, I saw him swimming over to me. I didn't think fast enough to gather everything up and slip out the side door. I froze with a coffee cup in one hand and a cinnamon roll in the other. Bud got right up over me and glared down with a weird kind of creepy half smile/smirk on his face. He motioned for me to step away from the pastry and out into the hallway. I didn't know whether I was going to get yelled at, hugged, or told a national secret. The conversation went something like this.

"I've been watching you," he snorted. "Tommy Trojan said you could be our next super star." Then he leaned in even closer, took his granny glasses (the ones that hung on the gold chain like my grandma's), and poked me in the chest with them.

"Let me ask you a question young man...do you ever read?"

I thought it was a trick question. I went brain dead. I did read many of the finer periodicals such as Sports Illustrated and Penthouse, but I knew he was referring to actual books, which I rarely read, but didn't care to admit to. I knew I had to give him an answer, so I mumbled, "Sure, yeah."

"Have you ever read the book, *Think and Grow Rich,* by Napoleon Hill?"

I shook my head, no. He poked me again with the damn granny glasses and said, "Okay, I'll tell ya what you need to do. There's a bookstore in Encino, down on the boulevard. Drive there today or tomorrow and buy that book. I want you to read it, okay?"

I nodded my head obediently and he swam away quietly.

*   *   *

Three weeks had elapsed since Bud Cole had hunted me down in the break room and ordered me to purchase *Think and Grow Rich,* which I did the very day he asked me to.

The first time through the book I was amazed at what I was reading. My mother, Helen, had always told me that I could *do* anything and *be* anything I truly desired to do or be. It was great when she'd tell me that. It always made me feel better, but then again, she was my mother. She was supposed to say crap like that. But this mysterious stranger, Napoleon Hill, he was now speaking to me via the book, telling me the same thing. But not only that, he was actually telling me *how* I could do and be all those things.

During my second pass through the book I made notes, but I didn't make them in the book, I made them on a yellow pad because I felt like writing in that book would be like defacing the Mona Lisa. The notes I made helped me absorb the lessons that applied to where I was at. During my third read through, I started memorizing and internalizing some of Napoleon Hill's sayings, the ones I knew would come in handy.

"The only limitation is that which one sets up in one's own mind."

"Failure cannot cope with persistence."

"Whatever the mind of man can conceive and believe it can achieve."

"Both poverty and riches are the offspring of thought."

That book made me believe that I could be a multi-millionaire. That book began to change my life.

Bud waltzed over to where I was standing, which was next to Larry Story. Larry turned and ran. I assumed he didn't want to get chewed out about his long hair, which he hadn't cut. Bud had that crooked, disturbing half smile on his face again. He began his interrogation.

"Young man, I asked you to go buy a book and read it a few weeks ago. Do you recall that conversation?"

What I wanted to say was, "It's a little too soon for me to have senile dementia, so, yeah, I recall the conversation," but what I said was, "Yessir."

"So, did you pick up that book, the one called *Think and Grow Rich*?"

"Yes, Bud, I did."

"You did?" He asked that with a small hint of surprise in his voice.

"Did you have a chance to start reading it yet?"

"Yessir. I'm on my third time through," I replied.

Bud stepped back, cocked his head like he'd gotten an answer he didn't expect to hear and started chewing on the corner of those damn granny glasses. I could tell that he didn't completely believe me. In a later conversation he admitted to that. In fact, he told me that only a third of the people he suggested the book to actually purchased it and read it. He also told me that NOBODY had ever read the book three times in the first two weeks they owned it.

He began a different level of interrogation. This one went a little deeper. His further cross-examination included a pop quiz on what I thought about a particular chapter, what specific points I thought I could apply to becoming a top salesperson. Again, he was testing me—trying to see if I was lying. He wanted to know exactly what I took away from the book. When he was satisfied with my rather long-winded answers, he smiled, folded up those damn glasses and started poking me in the chest again. He whispered to me like he was passing on a CIA secret. What he said to me next has stuck with me forever.

"Joe, in five years from now you'll be a product of the books you read and the people you associate with. So choose both of them carefully."

It was early and I wasn't fully awake so I simply nodded my head to placate him, hoping he'd stop poking me in the chest with his granny glasses. He patted me on he back and walked away.

> **"Joe, in five years from now you'll be a product of the books you read and the people you associate with. So choose both of them carefully."**

His counsel steeped in my brain for a long while before I completely understood what it meant. It marinated for months and change was gradual, but as my momentum of reading increased, I began to take note of things that came out of my mouth, statements and comments that even surprised me. I was becoming a product of the books I read. After I read two dozen more books on the subjects of positive mental attitude, sales, personal growth, communication and success, I began to notice that I could carry on a conversation at a much higher level with people that were substantially older than me and possessed far more formal education.

I also began to take note of a pervasive feeling that came over me when I was around certain people. People who were negative for the sake of being negative began to repel me. People that had no established direction or goals became less interesting to me. I found myself avoiding people, both in my personal and professional life, that didn't represent the right kind of connection for me. I assessed (both consciously and unconsciously), who actually aligned with where I wanted to go in my life and who could be supportive of those goals. As a result of shifting away from contact with certain types of people and towards other more conducive connections, I began to think, act and speak the language of top performers.

Again, it was all very gradual, but Bud was right. I did become a *product* of my input and the people I chose to associate with. If I'd known that, on that morning in the break room, Bud had handed me the combination to a safe full of riches, I would have kissed him on the lips...maybe not, but almost everything good in my life has come directly, or indirectly, from reading!

My original copy of *Think and Grow Rich* is dog-eared—completely worn out...pages falling out. The original book hasn't left my side in forty years. I've been turning those pages for that long. I keep it in my office closet in a plastic bag. The price tag is still on the book.

The book cost me $3.00.

I think I may have gotten my money's worth.

Before Bud Cole approached me that day in 1979, I had never read a self-help book. Napoleon Hill's, *Think and Grow Rich*, turned me on to a universe where anything I could imagine achieving was possible. I became a voracious reader and an eager student of the mind. I studied the thought processes and belief systems that separated top salespeople and leaders (Pareto's 20%) from all the rest. I soon learned that much of a top performers' success could be attributed to how they managed their thoughts, feelings, and responses. In short, their success was mainly about the *attitudes* they settled on and the behavioral habits they developed and practiced.

After Bud unlocked my thirst for reading and knowledge, I was soon able to assemble a list of concepts, philosophies, and thought processes that would become instrumental in my path to wealth. Over the years, I've read over eleven hundred books on subjects relating to sales, leadership, success, entrepreneurialism, and investing. That first book, *Think and Grow Rich*, was the catalyst. It was the foundation that ushered in an entirely different set of thoughts and outlooks for my life.

Knowing how successful people tick would become critical in my ability to overcome obstacles and *survive*, and then *thrive* in sales. My path wasn't a perfect line of ascension. There'd be severe tests of my commitment and fortitude in the near future. Things would happen to me eventually that would shake me to my core. The things I'm referencing were crushing losses and emotional setbacks that I hope you don't ever have to deal with. Without the foundation of reading and the right associations I would have never made it. I would've simply been another one of those people who tried the entrepreneurial world or outside commission sales and quit. I would have been one of those losers who walk around mumbling, "Yeah, the people that make it big are lucky or know somebody."

There was no way I was ever going to be that guy.

Reading helped me understand that I alone, was responsible for where I would wind up in the world.

Nobody else.

Bud's final comment to me that day, "In five years from now you'll be a product of the books you read and the people you associate with. So choose both of them carefully," was prophetic. By the mid 1980s I would become such a precise product of what I read and who I associated with that I didn't even recognize myself anymore.

But that's a story for another time.

THE INCREDIBLE LESSONS

Forgive my verbosity with regard to the lessons from this chapter, but reading did so much for me that I want to make sure I share all of it with you.

✓ **Reading opened up POSSIBILITIES for me:**

I wasn't born with a silver spoon in my mouth; it was more like one of those plastic **spork** things you get at a fast food place. My parents didn't have a lot of money and nobody in my family had ever made a great deal of income. As a result of my scripting and childhood environment, **I had no idea what was possible** and what I was capable of achieving. Reading *Think and Grow Rich* changed all of that. Napoleon Hill opened my mind up to what was possible, even if I was born on the *wrong* side of the tracks. I read stories about people rising from nothing to attain great wealth and accomplishment. **I began to realize what I might be capable of doing**. I stopped making excuses. I started to believe I could achieve something great in my life.

✓ **Reading made me more CONFIDENT:**

When I began to read, I also began to **feel better about myself**. I began to believe that **I had an *edge*** over people that were NOT reading, regardless of their many formal degrees. I knew a few things they didn't. This small advantage was enough for me to begin **feeling** and **acting** more **confident**, which in turn, spawned many other benefits.

✓ **Reading made me a DEEPER thinker:**

When you read **long-form** writing, you're digesting raw material, static words on paper or a screen. This forces you to **form your own thoughts** and mental pictures. It also powers you to **find connections in the words**. When you're reading, you're studying someone else's thought process, so **you must analyze what you're taking in** and **build arguments** in your head. Bottom line, reading helped me learn **how to *think* and *analyze*** on a much more profound level.

✓ **Reading DIFFERENTIATED me:**

As my confidence rose and I began to speak and *act* more **profoundly, people took notice of me.** People in my hierarchy singled me out and asked me to speak on subjects at Monday morning meetings. When they decided to add another Field Trainer or Unit Manager, I was the **obvious choice** for the promotion. Think about it, if you can *communicate* better, or point to a historical event you've read about and *elucidate* on it, **the more interesting and attractive you'll be** to those of influence. You will **stand out** from those that aren't reading.

✓ **Reading expanded my VOCABULARY:**

I've been accused of using too many big words (and I imagine I do), however when you're reading, you come across **words**, **phrases** and **nuances**, things you wouldn't see or hear in the normal course of your life. Reading expands your perspective, your vocabulary and **the way you talk**. Bottom line, when you read, you start *sounding* **more intelligent.**

✓ **Reading taught me how to tell STORIES:**

In sales, telling stories to *illustrate* and *cement* your point is an invaluable skill. Learning how to tell a story properly is developed through seeing **how others tell their stories**. Reading, whether it's a work of fiction, or a real-life story, can teach you how to tell a great story.

✓ **Reading improved my JUDGMENT:**

There is research that compares the general knowledge of **readers** to those who only **watch television** or **view videos**. Both formats offer input and new ideas, however the conclusions of the research showed a **stark difference** in respect to the intellectual outcome of both. Readers not only knew more than television/video watchers, but they were also **better at deciphering misinformation**.

Here's why...

When you read, you have to use certain **cognitive facilities** that you **don't** have to use when you're watching television or a video. *Watching* something is a completely *passive* activity. You're just sitting there, taking it in. The act of reading is a much more *vigorous* practice. It requires your **PARTICIPATION**. You're constantly *evaluating* the content against the body of what you already know, hence you must use those **cognitive judgment muscles**, and they **strengthen** as a result.

✓ **Reading improved my PEOPLE skills:**

This may seem counterintuitive. You may ask, "How could that be possible if your head is shoved into a book?"

Here's how it works; when you're reading novels, history or memoirs, you see all of the **personalities** fleshed out, and if the writer is good, you're getting **inside their head**. You're *seeing* what they're *thinking* and what their **motivations** are. This practice **expands your understanding of human nature** and what makes people tick. You'll see life through a different lens. You'll note how people *interact* within a situation or scenario. It may be a similar situation to one you have encountered, but you note that they connected in a totally different way.

As I began to **widen my reference** of how people could and did react, I was able to see things not just one way, but appreciate—**and even predict**—many different reactions and responses and not be alarmed or taken off-guard by them. Reading helped me better **understand the base motivations** people have, and in turn, this improved the way I was able to **CONNECT** with them and help them.

   ✓ **Reading helped me become a
    better COMMUNICATOR:**

When you read well-written long-form books, you begin to *reflect* what you read. I actually began to *imitate* and *emulate* what I read. What I was reading began to heavily influence my own writing and speaking skills. Good writers can say things *succinctly*. If you absorb this practice you will start to gain the ability to **say things *clearer* and *faster***, which in this sound-bite world, can be a very handy skill. This is especially true if your living depends on getting someone's time and attention. Reading also helped me learn how to ***think on my feet*** better. When I read books I'm always asking, "What's the communication methodology this author's employing? What's making this book actually *work*?"

✓ **Reading helped me RELAX and learn how to FOCUS:**

When Bud Cole poked me in the chest and told me to go buy the book, he also told me to read for **at least 15 minutes each morning** when I woke up and to read **15 minutes each night** before I went to bed. His suggestion stuck. When I brought that first book home from the bookstore, I opened it up and began to read it. It was after dinnertime and I read the book until I fell asleep that night. I woke up the next morning and started where I left off. In fact, I didn't just read for 15 minutes, I began to form the habit of reading for 30 – 45 minutes each morning. My hypothesis was that because I barely graduated from high school, wasn't planning to attend college, and wasn't as smart as most of my friends, **I'd need to double up**. Reading in the morning put good, **productive** and **positive** thoughts **in my head**. Those thoughts created crazy-good **energy** and **power** inside of my mind and body. By 8:00 a.m. I was ready to hit the field and conquer my world.

Bud Cole also told me that if I read before I went to bed at night it would help me relax. Reading slows down your brain and **gets it focused**. If you're in sales or leadership, **it's really hard to turn your brain off**. You re-hash everything that happened during your workday and everything you didn't get done. You sit and stew. The great thing about reading in the evening is that **it moves your thinking away from**

current problems and scenarios. You're magically pulled into **another world**. Your brain becomes focused on something else, usually something positive. There was a recent study that compared reading to other stress relievers like walking, listening to music, or drinking a cup of tea. Reading was found to be **the most effective**. It worked to lower heart rates and **relieved stress** in as few as **SIX MINUTES**.

✓ **Reading kept me young and USEFUL to my organization:**

Some say older people make better entrepreneurs and leaders. They typically have advantages in terms of their knowledge, experience and contacts. However, younger people that **passionately read** can also **LEVERAGE these same advantages**.

If you are older, research suggests that reading helps us **stay mentally sharp** as we age. Getting older and staying *in the game* can be a real challenge. We probably all know people who suffer from senile dementia or Alzheimer's and it's a frightening disease. Living to an older age is only a good thing if the **quality of your life** is good. It has been proven that **reading helps you form new connections of thought**. It helps you stay RELEVANT. Think about it, when you're reading new books, you're automatically receiving the **latest and greatest information**. Your brain will (by default), receive new content and associations.

In addition to helping your brain stay young, reading will assist you in becoming **more useful** to the people you serve. If you're a leader you know that part of the game is about keeping your team **focused** on the same boring set of

Competencies, **Attitudes** and **Pipeline** practices that we know they must stay dedicated to. The problem is that we can begin to sound like a *broken record* if we simply harp on **the same tired, old stuff** without *conveying it* with some **new twist**, repackaged with fresh, cutting edge deliverables. As I progressed through the executive sales leadership ranks, I worked my butt off to find new information, methods and strategies to wrap around the principles that we *never* deviated from.

If I hadn't continued reading...a lot...I wouldn't have had the right **INPUT** to create fresh, innovative **OUTPUT** for my team, as I became a leader. **I would have sounded flat—** like many uninspired managers do—and I would have lost influence over my team.

CHAPTER THIRTEEN

Comfort Food

"No man is useless while he has a friend."
—ROBERT LOUIS STEVENSON, Scottish novelist & poet

T here are two things I really appreciate in a friend or mentor.
First, I value a person who can simply *listen* to you, when
you're screwing up, or you're in pain. (Too many so-called
leaders feel the requirement to *pontificate* or lecture) Secondly, I
appreciate someone who can make really good fried chicken. One
evening, in late 1979, those two talents intersected providing me
some much-needed comfort food. In addition, the treasured example
of true leadership I'll tell you about in this chapter would come to
be a tool I used many times over in my career as a mentor and coach.

Like me, Tom Smith enjoyed food. On our periodic days working
together in the field, we'd carefully plan the most efficient sales
route, but also chart out a geographic path strategically aimed at the

best greasy spoons in Los Angeles. We'd actually get as excited about a good lunch as we did about selling a ton of business.

By this juncture I'd been selling those $39.00 accident policies for about six months, which was a lot longer than most people stayed around Trans Pacific. Also by this time, Tom had become someone I deeply admired. Even today, as I think about his influence on me at such a young age, it's hard for me to articulate the impact the relationship had on my life. He was the first person to take me under his wing and offer true mentorship. Tom had also become an authentic friend. He taught me how to sell, but a lot of people could have done that.

He did more than that.

Tom taught me how to be a real *professional*. He was just as concerned about my personal life as my professional one. He often echoed my father by saying things like, "If you're man enough to stay out late and drink, you ought to be man enough to show up to work the next morning."

We only had to have that discussion twice.

Tom had sold bowling balls on the road for Brunswick before landing in the insurance game with Penn Life. He and his lovely wife, Sylvia, lived in a tastefully furnished condo in the San Fernando Valley. They were both on their second marriage, all their kids grown and gone. Tom was old school in the very best traditions and principles of sales and sales leadership. He was a salesman's salesman. As John Maxwell would later write, "You have to KNOW the way, SHOW the way and GO the way." Tom knew all three of those better than anyone I knew. His pitch and closing skills were sugary sweet, just like his smile, and that trademark grin of his never left his face regardless of what occurred around him. He was unflappable. He knew how to pick someone up and dust him or her off when they were down. He was also effusive in his praise of people in public, but he also knew when to take you aside, privately, and chew your ass out—but only when it was really warranted.

At that six-month benchmark with Trans Pacific, I was a 'tweener'—not a brand new rookie, but also not an established veteran either. The famous author, Robert Schuller, had created the, "Peak to Peek" principle. He suggested that you climb up on a high **peak**, you're exhausted, but feel like you've reached a certain respectable level. Then you get a **peek** at a higher peak—another level, and you desire to go there.

That's how the game of sales is.

Regardless of how well you think you're doing in your own little bubble, you can always point to someone who's doing a little better, and it pisses you off because you're not there! Personal pride and competitive juices kick in and you want to reach the production level they're at. If it isn't that *internal* thing chewing away at you, it can be the *external* pressure some companies put on you. You prove that you can produce at one level, and they want you to do just a little bit more.

At that juncture, I had a little money in my pocket, so I started to screw off a little. My activity level dropped and production results were trending down. I was having victories, but was also feeling a little beat up. Logically, I knew I needed to hang in there, find my energy again, pump the pump and get back into the top five on the leader board. There was another part of me that simply wanted to *bail out* on the gig. It was damn hard work and my emotional gas tank was low.

So I was moving in the general direction of Quitsville.

I dropped the coin in the slot of the payphone. I was calling in my daily activity and production numbers to Tom. Of course, there were no cell phones in 1979, so I'd scramble to find a public phone each evening and hit Tom's home number. If he didn't answer, I'd leave my results on his tape machine.

It was my hope that Tom didn't answer that night, and I'd be able to leave a message on his tape machine.

He answered.

I gave him my numbers that evening…ZERO for something…I think he heard it in my voice and then, without thinking, I blurted it out.

"Tom, I'm not sure I wanna' do this any more. I'm running on empty. I've spent the last few days thinking about quitting."

He didn't skip a beat!

"Hey, Joe. You had a bad day. So what. I've felt like quitting sales a million times, but you are too talented and shouldn't make that kind of decision after a tough day. Look, where are you at right now? It's about five. Can you get to Reseda by six?" Then, without waiting for an answer, he asked, "You like fried chicken, right? Sylvia asked me to make my specialty for dinner. I got a sixer of Lowenbrau in the fridge. Get over here and we'll talk about what went wrong out there today. We'll get this fixed. And even if we can't, we'll eat some chicken and have a few cold beers."

Now, I have to tell you, I love fried chicken—I love fried anything—and I rarely turn down a homemade dinner in the first place, but, if you toss a sixer of complimentary cold ones on top of a free chicken dinner, then it's downright impossible for me to say no. I asked Tom for his home address and headed over. He mentioned that we were going to discuss what went wrong with my day, so I was curious of what he was going to say to try to talk me out of quitting.

I'd never been to Tom's home. I'd only hung out with him outside of the office at cocktail gatherings. I didn't know what to expect from a social/personal perspective. I knocked on the door of the condo. When he opened it, he was holding two ice-cold beers. He handed me one and clinked my bottle with his.

"Here's to a shitty day, Joe."

He snorted out a laugh with a big grin on his face. Then he took half his beer down in one gulp.

Tom was wearing a Hawaiian shirt, shorts and flip-flops. I'd never seen him without a suit and tie on. His attire instantly relaxed me. He introduced me to his wife, Sylvia. She gave me a big hug and welcomed me into their home. She commenced to tell me that she wished she had a dime for every time Tom got "skunked" in the field. Tom dispensed with formalities. He instructed me to roll a few pieces of chicken in the batter while he fished a few cooked pieces out of the boiling pot of oil. Then he told me to finish mashing the potatoes while he popped the cornbread into the oven.

I'd only been in their home a few minutes and I was already on full kitchen duty—part of the family! We dragged our drinks and plates of chicken out to the couch; Sylvia made herself a martini, flipped on the TV and dialed in the Laker game. Chick Hearn called the game as we wolfed down some of the tastiest fried chicken I'd ever had, except for my mom's. I didn't want to over-stay my welcome, so when the game was over (and the six-pack of Lowenbrau was toast), I said my goodbyes. Sylvia gave me a hug on the way out the door and Tom followed me out, draping his arm around me.

"You're gonna' be a great salesman and a great trainer. We're gonna' build a team around you. That's the plan. Let's go get 'em tomorrow. Put in the numbers with a smile on your face and the sales will follow. Good things are right around the corner for you, Joe."

I was waiting for more, but there wasn't any more.

That's all he said to me.

It was then, as I walked to my car, that I realized we hadn't discussed business at all that night. During the two hours we were together, I'd tried to bring up the issue of business several times. I'd started to tell him how crappy my day and week was when we were cooking the chicken, but the subject somehow got changed. Sylvia would interrupt me and ask me about my family or Tom would remark on how lousy the Lakers were playing. Every time I tried to bitch about my day, one of them would laugh it off and change the subject.

On my drive home I realized that he didn't invite me over to have me reiterate how shitty my day was. He got it. He'd personally had a million shitty days like mine in his long career. He didn't ask me to come over so he could pontificate, or display his vast knowledge of sales or leadership.

Tom simply invited me over because he knew I needed a friend.

He knew I needed someone who understood, somebody to reach in and pull me out of the murky water. Tom knew that I also needed to feel a part of something more—something more significant than simply walking down the street and selling accident policies. Tom, like any great leader, knew just what I needed that night.

But more importantly, he knew what I *didn't* need.

I had an amazing plate of fried chicken that evening, but the real comfort food was Tom and Sylvia's warmth and laughter. The real comfort food was their willingness to open up their home and invite me in, like I was family. That sincere gesture spoke more to me than anything else Tom could have said. After that evening, things changed from an emotional connection standpoint. I wasn't only working hard for myself; I was working hard not to let Tom down. I couldn't let a guy down that believed in me that much and would take me into his home and treat me like family.

I had a better day the next day. I refocused on the numbers (with a smile on my face) and wrote a ton of business.

And yes, Tom was right, good things were around the corner for me.

I became a consistently high producer—getting back into the top five spots on the production board again. More importantly, within five months time from that homemade chicken dinner I'd be given the chance to become the youngest sales manager (at age 19) that PennCorp and Trans Pacific had ever promoted!

Since that late fall evening in '79, I've paid this forward many times over. I never made fried chicken for people. I knew I could never make it as well as my mother or Tom Smith. My specialty was spaghetti and red sauce. When I sensed someone was down and needed a hand, I'd start boiling the water and I'd invite them over. When they'd arrive, I'd make sure I met them in the driveway with two glasses of red wine or a cold one. I wouldn't pontificate about solutions to their problems. They didn't need a lecture, just as I didn't, forty years prior. I wouldn't allow them to wallow knee deep in their own muddy waters either. I'd just serve them a plate of spaghetti, another glass of red wine and then put on a game and comment on how crappy the Lakers or Dodgers were playing.

They just needed a friend.

They just needed to know that they were part of something bigger.

All they needed was a little comfort food.

THE INCREDIBLE LESSONS

I think the leadership and mentorship lessons are fairly clear here. So we'll just leave this chapter alone, as it stands.

CHAPTER FOURTEEN

My Chili Dog Epiphany (Revisited)

"Mentors, by far, are the most important aspects of businesses."

—DAYMOND JOHN, entrepreneur, investor, TV personality

I've written about this unlikely experience (and the incredible lessons that emanated from it) once before. I mentioned this awesome episode in my first book, <u>The CAP Equation, A Foolproof Formula For Unlimited Success in Sales</u>. However, I'd like to go a little bit deeper on this unique experience in this book.

Mentors are all around you. Sometimes they're obvious, sometimes they're not. Sometimes they're assigned to you, and at other times you stumble across them. They can teach you many things, or just say one thing that sticks to you like Gorilla Glue. They can be in your life for a long time, or just a moment.

I was eleven months into my insurance career when I met another mentor.

He would only touch my sales career for a day.

By this time I'd turned a corner—figured things out. I'd conquered all of the key selling competencies necessary to survive and thrive in B2B sales. More importantly, I'd learned how to manage my emotions—I'd developed some great philosophies and attitudes that I used to manage that critical six inches between my ears. I was becoming a fairly solid and complete sales package, and had done so at a rather young age.

Bud Cole cornered me in the break room (yet again), one May morning in 1980. I had my perpetual donut in one hand and he had his customary granny glasses in his. He began to poke me in the chest as he lit up his conversation.

"Joe. We're adding a field trainer to Tom's team. You're going to be that field trainer. You're ready. We're going to start indoctrinating you into the role next week. Listen, you're going to spend a day in the field with John Jamelkowski before any formal promotion takes place."

He poked me in the chest and talked up Jamelkowski like he was the second coming of Jesus.

"You've met John. He's the best we have at the field training process. He's a damn machine. You're going to spend a day in the field with him. We want you to observe the *Polish Assassin* at work. Watch what he does and how he does it when you're out there with him. You soak up any wisdom you can. Ask him a lot of questions. Pick his brain—get him to tell you all about his training philosophies. You'll learn more in one day from him than most salespeople learn in their lifetime."

I nodded my head as Bud extolled the merits of being mentored by John Jamelkowski. It all sounded great and I was eager to hang out with the "Polish Assassin," but little did I know that this solitary day with John over thirty-eight years ago would yield a lesson (a sound bite), that would take less than thirty seconds, but provide a way of thinking that would last a lifetime.

By the way, Bud never *asked* me if I wanted to be a field trainer, he *told* me. That's how things worked around there. We didn't discuss the particulars of the promotion; I never asked him how or why I was selected. I simply went to Tom and asked him how people got promoted. He matter of factly stated, "Hey, you've been here almost a year. They promote anyone that makes it a year."

Tom's response made me feel special.

Not!

Tom told me that I would be signing a field-training contract and I'd receive a small override on the people that he assigned to me for training. Tom also filled me in a little more about John. He confirmed that the dude was truly a machine. John piloted F-4 Phantoms in Vietnam, which, obviously, required a great deal of concentration and attention. After Lieutenant Jamelkowski retired from active service in the Air Force he applied all of that same focus, all of his disciplines, to his new chosen field, insurance sales. Tom told me that John was meticulous in his preparation and approach to his work, just as if he was going through a preflight checklist. Tom hinted that being in the field with John would be different than when he and I were in the field together. He described John as "Not a very talkative guy." That dubious description left me thinking, "If he wasn't a very talkative guy, how was I going to learn anything?"

Bud gave me the address to John's office. It was a little hole in the wall in Camarillo, California. Camarillo is a small town, about forty minutes northwest of Van Nuys, just inland from the beach. I was told by Bud to be there at 7:45 a.m., "sharp." I arrived a few minutes late because of traffic. John was pacing when I opened the door. He looked up.

"Good morning young man. We are already a few minutes behind schedule. Let's get moving."

I noticed that John's office was not large or ornate, but it was neat. Every shelf and drawer was labeled and everything seemed to have a place. He had his sight seller open and was filling it with instant issue Safe Drivers policies. He had a Thomas Guide open to a certain page, and a photocopy of that same page with a route marked in red pen laid next to it. He turned the pages in his well-worn sight seller, like he was looking for anything that may be out of place. I didn't speak while 'Rain Man' focused on his routine.

Neither did he.

Finally, he finished checking over his sight seller, closed it and simply motioned for the door. I followed him out as he locked it and we made our way to his Cadillac, El Dorado.

Tom's description of Jamelkowski as "not a very talkative guy" was an understatement for sure. He was more or less a Tibetan monk. He made me aware that our first stop on his cold call route would be in Saticoy, and that we'd make our way back to Camarillo for the second half of the day. That was the extent of our conversation on the ten-minute ride to Saticoy. He had the oldies station on and when I started to make small talk he reached over and turned the volume knob up. Needless to say, I didn't say much else on the ride.

I was afraid to.

He parked the Caddy and pointed his finger at a row of small retail shops. He started walking. All he said was, "We're going to hit all of these and then go to see a current policy holder." We marched from business door to business door, his eyes constantly focused on the person in front of him. He smiled and stayed right on script. It was the same script I'd learned from Sergeant Darnell eleven months earlier. He delivered it word for word. When his work was done with one prospect, win or lose, he'd smile again, shake a hand, turn, and walk out the door. There was no wasted emotion or energy, whether he wrote business or not, however he seemed to be writing business on every third or fourth approach.

What really blew me away was his ability to walk out of one door and within seconds, have another target locked into his crosshairs. He was making twice the number of approaches than I normally made in the same period of time. He could do this because there was zero wasted motion or emotion. There was no chit-chat, like, "Screw him," or "We really nailed that one." There were also no prejudgments being made by him. He never seemed to question if we should go into this business or that one. All of the doors were the same to him. There certainly weren't any smoke breaks or coffee breaks. In short, there was NOTHING but the relentless pursuit of sixty-plus walk-ins. He only stopped after each approach to take the Countdown to Success card out of his shirt pocket and cross out another number, or circle one that he'd presented or sold.

After we had walked into each and every available business on that block (and a few places that didn't turn out to be real businesses), he motioned towards the car.

"Let's go call on a customer ticket."

He wrote twelve units of additional business on the existing policyholder without breaking a sweat, and then we drove back towards Camarillo. There wasn't any small talk on the drive back. He turned the oldies station back on and hummed along to the Beatles. We hit every possible door in two more business parks that he'd pre-identified. It was almost 1:30 p.m. when he mumbled that is was, "Time for lunch." I was frigging starving. I was used to stopping for lunch around 11:45 a.m., so little Joey's tum-tum was on empty for sure. It was a grueling morning for me, and a profitable morning for John.

He had made more money in one morning than most of our deadbeat agents earned in a week!

I asked him how many walk-ins we had made and without glancing at the card he responded, "Forty-one including the customer ticket.

We talked to sixteen business owners, gave eleven presentations and wrote twenty-eight units of business including the existing account."

John Jamelkowski was indeed a machine; one that was on target to make the most cold calls I'd ever seen in one day. He was also on target to write the most units of new business I'd ever seen produced in one day. That said, you couldn't tell by his facial expressions that he was tearing it up, because there were none.

For our lunch he chose an outdoor hot dog stand near the office. He pointed to the menu board and instructed, "Order the chili dogs with everything." I did.

I ordered one. He got three.

He began mowing down the gut rockets like he hadn't eaten in a month. John was halfway done with his third dog before I finished my first. Somewhere in between chomps of my leaky dog, I recalled that I was supposed to soak up some wisdom and "ask a lot of questions." I was to pick his brain—get him to tell me all about his training philosophies. How do you do that when a guy doesn't stop working long enough so that you can ask? I decided to choke out a question while we were eating. This guy didn't take many breaks, and I wasn't sure I'd get another chance.

"John, can I ask you a little bit about training and retaining new agents—what your philosophies are on the subject?"

This can be a complex question. Most accomplished sales managers and trainers would take an opportunity like this to pontificate—run off at the mouth. They would want to impress the new guy with all that they knew on the subject. Based on what I'd experienced with John that morning, I wasn't expecting him to dish out a long dissertation, but I also didn't anticipate the extreme brevity he used to answer my question.

His answer came fast and hard.

It was succinct and unadorned.

John said it this way:

"If you hire a new agent and they're failing to produce, the problem is one or more of only three possible causes. Either they're not *saying* or *doing* the right *things*, or they're not saying or doing them the right *way*. If the're doing both of those things well and they are still struggling, then they're not seeing enough people." He paused to sip his Coke.

"It's as simple as that, buddy boy."

"Burrrrrrrrrp."

"Selling is basically a math problem."

And that was it. He jammed the rest of his last dog into his mouth. He was done talking and already moving towards his car.

John had distilled his entire coaching and training model down to three elements. In his opinion, these three factors were the root causes for all failure in commission sales. Apparently, these were the three things he focused on when training new insurance agents. In John's mind, if those three factors were checked off the flight plan, then the plane would get up in the air, hit the intended target and land on the ground safely. There was no luck involved in John's selling process—there was none needed. Luck wasn't what a fighter pilot depended on for a successful mission.

John made sure his agents developed proficiencies—that they were competent. To him "saying and doing the right things" meant that they knew how to present and close. Then he'd make sure they adopted the right thought processes and attitudes. Those mind-sets equated to the "right way" that he referenced. He'd then inspect their activity level—the "enough people" thing—making sure they made sixty walk-ins a day.

John Jamelkowski had abridged the complicated business of sales training to those three factors. The sales process wasn't some convoluted, emotional, or psychological mystery to him. It was a checklist, a simple math problem, and one that he already knew how to solve.

That small sound bite between bites of the chilidogs in 1980 was virtually all of the insight I'd ever need to make a great living as a manager of salespeople. The words would even enable me to become rich, but I didn't know any of that at the time. I took in the lesson that day, but it took me a few weeks to sort through it all, fully comprehend it, and re-purpose it in my own style and for my own application.

Because I believe in R & D (robbing and duplicating), I began to claim the first part of his lesson—his mantra—as my own refrain:

Say and do the right *things*.

Say and do them the right *way*.

Say them to *enough* people.

For years after that I would coach salespeople, using this uncomplicated way of thinking. It also evolved into my go-to sales training methodology over the years. Then as I grew into a more corporate role, one that pulled me farther and farther away from the front lines of sales, I had less opportunity to teach about this method. I had even fewer opportunities to tell the story about John and the Chilidogs.

The story faded into the alcoves of my memory.

I hadn't told it in many, many years.

Then, in the spring of 2014, the ageless conversation with John entered my headspace again. I was sitting at my writing desk staring at the screen of my MacBook Pro, looking at the working manuscript of my first non-fiction book. I was stalled out to some degree—stalled on a great title and theme for the book. I closed my eyes and replayed the meaningful chilidog conversation in my head, trying to evoke his words that day. I hadn't told the story in a decade, but for some reason my recall became amazingly sharp. The last little part of his lecture slapped me right in the face. His mic drop statement.

"Selling is basically a math problem."

There it was!

The "math problem" line was my clue to package the content in the way of a math equation or formula. The job of making my manuscript come to life was as simple as codifying the advice John gave me that day, thirty-four years earlier.

I grabbed a yellow pad and began to categorize what the "right things" are—the basic skills that a salesperson will always need to learn. I entitled this grouping Competencies. The "right way" was less tangible. These are more or less behavioral patterns—an overall mind-set. For this element I chose the tagline, Attitudes. "Enough of the right people" means lead generation and lead management practices, so I selected the word, Pipeline, as the label of this third and last component.

On the second page of my yellow pad I wrote out the mathematical equation:

$$C + A \times P = \textbf{Unlimited Success in Sales}$$

I'd been teaching the three critical causes of success in commission sales for over three decades, calling them "the right things, the right way and to enough of the right people." I'd been teaching them independently of each other, but had never connected them in a programmed manner. When you do form them into a calculation, it demonstrates how vitally dependent these three areas are on each other, just like a mathematical equation! After all said and done, 1 + 0 is never going to equal 2!

With that epiphany, The CAP Equation© was born and I had a title for my first book on the subject of the sales process. It turned out that the day in the field with John Jamelkowski was the gift that kept on giving.

On that auspicious Tuesday in May of 1980, John worked me into exhaustion. He didn't turn me loose until after 6:00 p.m. We made over seventy cold calls that day, wrote more new business than I'd ever seen written by a Penn Life agent, before or after. John said very little, but his work habits, focus and disciplines said it all. He was simply the most focused cold calling instrument of death I'd ever witnessed.

I lost track of John after I moved on from Trans Pacific and PennCorp. I went one way and he went another. With no cell phones or social media it wasn't uncommon to lose touch with people in those ancient times. Our paths did cross one more time in the early '90s. I was a newly promoted regional sales manager for a company called, Aflac. John was selling high-dollar life insurance plans to key executives. We ran into each other in the lobby of a building on Ventura Boulevard. John had heard of some of my failures and successes through the coconut telegraph and made reference to some specifics of my career. He looked genuinely happy to see me, but he glanced at his watch—seeming to be preoccupied.

In that hurried moment I tried to summon the words to express to him how much that one day in the field meant to me—how impactful his words and mentorship had been for me. He shrugged his shoulders. I don't think he really got it, or maybe he was just so humble that he didn't want to take any credit for anything. Funny, he didn't seem to remember the conversation we had over the chilidogs, but he did recall his sales results from our day in the field together. As we stood there in the lobby he recounted exactly how many walk-ins we made, the number of presentations, closes and units of business we sold. He recalled those obscure facts because those things were important to him.

As John was shaking my hand, trying to break free from the conversation and get to his next appointment, he said something. He had a smile on his face. He rarely wasted a smile.

"That *was* a great day wasn't it?"

I couldn't begin to tell him how stupid great it really was for me, so I didn't try. I simply smiled back, nodded my head, and let him go. He was busy. He had to go make another presentation.

John passed away a few months later. I was shocked when I heard this news. He looked fine when I ran into him a few months earlier. The broker John worked for told me that he'd been sick for a while— brain tumor. He'd been pronounced terminal months earlier, but he'd opted to keep working. He knew his fate the last time I bumped into him, but he never brought it up.

Guys like John didn't make their problems yours.

He was a rare breed.

Mentors are all around you if you're looking for them. They aren't always the person directly assigned to you. Sometimes they just happen and you better be ready. They can say really significant things that can change your way of thinking and your career if you're listening. These magical mentors can sometimes only be in your life for a day, but they can cause you to have an epiphany that feeds you for a lifetime.

So, that's what happened to me one spring day in 1980.

Bud was right.

I'd learned more from John in that one day than most salespeople and leaders learn in their entire lifetime.

THE INCREDIBLE LESSONS

Like I said at the outset of this chapter, I've written about John and the Chilidog epiphany before. My objective with this book goes beyond just telling the story. In this volume of work I have the luxury to draw your attention to all of the great *nuggets* imbedded in this story. Let's take the time to unpack all of them so you don't miss any.

✓ **Sometimes you CHOOSE a specific path, sometimes IT chooses YOU:**

I was cruising along fine when Bud told me I was "selected" to be a field trainer. It's not like I had a grand career plan nicely penned out on paper, and this promotion was part of that plan. Nothing like that was going on at all. In fact, if they didn't pick me to be a field trainer, **I probably would have never considered stepping into a management role**. After all, I had just survived my first full year in commission sales; I was doing fine and had zero responsibilities. Why complicate my life, right?

As soon as I got into the position of field trainer, I learned that I possessed some natural gifts in the areas of recruiting, coaching, leadership and organizational development. I've focused most of my career in those areas. The skill-sets that I began to learn and refine in 1980 helped me earn millions during my long career. I want to make sure you don't miss this...**if a mentor sees something in you and wants to promote your career, it's probably not an accident** and you probably shouldn't fight it.

And...oh, NOTHING is an *accident*.

✓ **Mentors can be UNLIKELY people:**

Sometimes **they don't look like you.** I wasn't drawn to John. In fact, prior to spending the day in the field with him, I'd barely spoken to him. He didn't seem like a guy I'd have a beer with. **I** *prejudged* **him**—put him in some kind of box. I perceived him as stuffy, not friendly or helpful. That wasn't true at all. He was simply very disciplined and focused. If Bud Cole hadn't forced me to spend a day in the field with him, I'm sure I wouldn't have spent any time with him at all...and **I would have missed so much.** He was an **unlikely** mentor. We shouldn't prejudge anyone. If somebody is a top performer, it is to our benefit to **EXTEND ourselves** and try to **make a meaningful** *connection* with that person.

✓ **ACTIONS do SPEAK (and teach) louder than words:**

Many sales managers or leaders like the sound of their own voice—they like to pontificate. John was the **antithesis** of that. John was not a man of many words. He liked to **SHOW people the way**. He was a person of **action**. I'm sure John could have sat me down in his office, kicked back in his chair till noon and talked my ear off about his philosophies, mindsets, beliefs strategies, etc., but that's not the way he was wired. Because he was a man of action, many of the people he coached and trained also became committed to doing the work.

✓ **You can run long and hard when your EMOTIONS are under control:**

Because John allowed for no **wasted** emotion (and motion), in his daily regime, he could work longer and harder than most people. He had taught himself to **detach** from any emotion that would **subtract gas** from his emotional tank. He didn't allow **energy vampires** of any kind to invade his brain or body. He didn't *celebrate* too long when he had a win, and he sure as heck didn't spend a lot of time *mourning* what didn't go well. As a result, he was able to **CHANNEL 100% of his energy** into another face-to-face selling opportunity. He knew that wasted emotion and motion only **slowed the progress** toward his sacred goals.

✓ **Most great philosophies are CLEAN and easy to explain:**

I'm not going to focus on WHAT John said. Instead I want you to focus on the WAY in which John said it—the **economy** of John's **delivery of his thoughts**. He had a very simple and clean understanding of why salespeople failed, and also why they didn't. His beliefs were so unassuming that they could have been easily missed. Focus on the **efficient manner** he used in his explanation of his philosophies. Since that day, and over the years, I've learned if somebody needs a whole lot of words to explain a concept, it probably isn't well-baked in their oven, and it is probably only a **theory**—and an unproven one at that.

John worked hard to get his thinking clean and to explain his viewpoints succinctly. Great salespeople and great leaders do that. John was way ahead of his time. Now, more than ever before, if you want to earn the time and attention of a prospect (or the people you lead), you have to say it CONCISELY.

✓ **Sales pros (and great coaches) don't rely on LUCK. They see sales as a MATH problem:**

John was **PRECISE**. He had his pitch and rebuttals down cold. He had his emotions 100% under control, his **management of his primetime** was spotless, and he knew his **numbers** and **conversion ratios** well. John never counted on luck and none was needed. John looked at sales as a mathematical equation—you know what to say and ask—you smile and dial—and you talk to enough people and follow up with them properly. He was a machine. **He put all of the pressure on the system**—the numbers—and because of that he could *transfer* what he did in the field to others. He removed their excuses, justifications, rationalizations and all of the other BS stuff that new salespeople can gravitate to. Because of his logical, **systems based approach**, he never had to get involved in conversations about territory, lack of experience, luck etc.

CHAPTER FIFTEEN

My 10,000 Hours

"When you are not practicing, someone else is getting better."

—ALLEN IVERSON, former NBA player

After spending the day with John Jamelkowski, I signed my first management contract. I was handed a box of business cards that proclaimed I was a "Sales Manager" and in late May of 1980 I hired my first salesperson. Well, actually, Tom Smith hired him and assigned him to me. He wound up quitting, but not right away, so at least I was able to *practice* on him for a while. The second hire went a little better, lasted a little longer, but also wound up quitting.

It was brutal.

I didn't quite understand it.

I'd been with PennCorp for a year, so trust me, I'd witnessed hundreds of people that quit, or had never gotten started.

But I wasn't their manager!

Now it was personal—their failure was mine. It was as if I had bombed when they quit, and I wasn't in the mood to crash and burn in the new role. I'd worked my way from a struggling newbie to a top producer—a star in that system. I was handed a management contract and told I was the youngest person that PennCorp had ever promoted to a sales management position. I was nineteen years old and feeling arrogant. There was no way I was going to do anything but tear it up. My plan was to set new records as a trainer, just like I did as an agent.

In my head, and on paper, it seemed easy. Because I was skilled at going down the street and opening new accounts, I'd be able to get others to do that in volume. However I was about to learn a valuable lesson. Just because you know how to do something well, it doesn't mean you automatically know how to transfer that thing to others. In fact, some of the best salespeople make horrible trainers and managers.

By the time I was *zero for four* in getting people successfully onboarded, I wasn't acting so conceited anymore. Some measure of humility kicked in. I had to remedy the situation and that would take two things. First, I had to drop the 'hot shit' facade and ask for some help—get some coaching. Secondly, I would have to become open again and be willing to continue putting in my 10,000 Hours.

If the "10,000 Hour" reference eludes you, I'll explain it. It is a theory that was first proffered by a Swedish psychologist named K. Anders Ericsson. It was popularized and brought into our everyday vocabulary by noted author, Malcolm Gladwell, in his 2008 book, *Outliers*. In *Outliers*, Gladwell looked at the factors that caused high levels of success. To support his argument, he examined how Bill Gates and The Beatles achieved their extreme success. He suggests that neither were an overnight sensation. Throughout his book,

Gladwell mentioned the "10,000 Hour Rule," asserting that the key to success in any endeavor is, to a large extent, a matter of *practicing* specific tasks for a total of 10,000 hours. There are people that swear by Gladwell's assumptions and also some doubters that debate the hypothesis.

From my perspective, the 10,000 Hour Rule is a very handy *standard*.

It gives a person new to their position a clear benchmark. It suggests the approximate amount of time they'll need to invest in their chosen craft to become somewhat expert at it. Of course, Mr. Gladwell published his book in 2008, eons after the period of time I'm writing about, so I actually practiced this rule not knowing it existed, or had a name. I knew instinctively that I had to keep working, refining and practicing my craft. I did this intuitively, never recognizing the approximate block of time as something *magical*. It wasn't until I'd semi-retired from my last executive level position and read Gladwell's book that I made a connection.

If you want to quantify what 10,000 hours really looks like, you would use the example of some crazy entrepreneur (like me or you), who works about seventy hours a week. (Let's use the number 67 hours per week) Now you might say, Joe B., few people work that many hours each week, however I can challenge that.

If you calculate an average number of hours spent in the field it's easily 32. Add to that the typical amount of hours spent in the office, let's say 15. We spend approximately 8 hours a week on the phone (conducting business), in the car on the way home. If we recognize the time spent at home, either thinking about our business, doing online research, or reading, it will easily add up to another 12 hours. When you add all of those hours up, it totals 67. This is a neat figure because if you take two weeks off a year and then multiply that 67 hour week × 50 weeks, × 3 years it adds up to your 10,000 hours.

So, borrowing from Anders and Malcolm, the hypothesis I'm suggesting is that it takes a hard working salesperson about 3 years to complete their 10,000 hours and become a master of their craft. If you think about it, it would be hard for anyone of average intelligence—who was also coachable—to think about, practice and refine any proven method for three solid years and not become pretty damn good at their job.

Malcolm Gladwell did not popularize the 10,000 Hour Rule until twenty-eight years after I'd begun practicing it. All I knew in 1980 was that I had to keep learning and grinding away at my craft. I knew I had to be willing to invest a massive amount of time in the practice of hiring, training and leading people. These were very different skill sets than the ones I'd spent the previous eleven months learning and becoming competent at. These would be new—and foreign—skills, ones that I would have to make a new commitment to learn, and I knew that it would be uncomfortable. But I also knew that I could win at the job of training salespeople, just like I won at the job of selling, if I made a decision to do exactly that.

When I read about Gladwell's 10,000 hours in 2008, my mind went "Bingo." He just put a definite number to my work ethic philosophy.

One of the first things I did was gather data from Bud and Tom. I wanted to know which field trainer had the biggest sales team in our region. I also wanted to know what the best agent retention rate was. There was a field trainer down in San Diego that had 13 active salespeople. Bud told me that this was the most people any field trainer was managing. I also knew that John Jamelkowski had the best retention rates of any trainer or full charge manager. For every 10 hires John made, approximately 8 would produce something. That means 2 people out of 10 would do all the work of getting an insurance license, then they would show up to basic training and learn the stupid script—survive sergeant Darnell's class, then they'd go out into the field and quit before they wrote 1 policy. That was so amazing to me that I had to ask Bud and Tom twice if the statistic was correct.

Out of the 8 agents that produced at least 1 policy, about 3 of them would leave the business within the first ninety days. That left

5 bodies still standing after one full quarter of tenure. Out of those 5, John would retain 3 productive agents past the 12-month mark. Of course, Jamelkowski had the BEST retention numbers. Tom was a close second, averaging 2.5 retained agents after 12 months. Tom's numbers were good, but retention averages fell off big time after that. The entire western region only averaged 2 retained agents out of 10 after the 1-year mark and most teams hovered closer to 1 or 1.5.

Those numbers blew me away, and not in a good way.

Again, I'd seen people come and go, but I'd never completely quantified the carnage. Bud reminded me about the Pareto Principle—the 80/20 Rule. I wrote about this extensively in my first book, *The CAP Equation*. Simply put, 80% of any *effect* will emanate from only 20% of the *cause*. For our purposes, 80% of all productivity will come from only 20% of the producers. This principle evolved from the writings of Vilfredo Pareto in the late 1800s. He proved his hypothesis over and over using different scenarios, but it always seemed to shake out. So, in my mind, I reasoned that the retention rate of the average trainer or manager wasn't any better than what would naturally happen if there were no trainer or manager in place at all.

Further, I got to thinking that the trainers and managers averaging LESS than 20% retention must have actually been doing something unhelpful—something that *sabotaged* their team growth and the development of their agents.

In short, they were actually *running off* their new agents!

Hence, my thinking was if I simply wasn't horrible to the agents assigned to me, I'd at least be an *average* trainer. Then, if I could emulate what better trainers and managers were doing (guys like Jamelkowski and Tom), I could inch towards a better retention number.

Now, I have to tell you that I am far from a math major, but if I could move from retaining 2 agents out of ten to getting 3 to stick around after a full 12-months, it wouldn't be an insignificant change of just 1 percentage point (the difference between 1 and 2); it would be a massive improvement of 33%. I would be doing 33% better than the average trainer—probably producing 33% more than the average team pound for pound. I also knew that if you compounded that better retention rate quarter-over-quarter and year-after-year, the team would explode exponentially.

I knew instinctively that I had to apply John Jamelkowski's mantra to sales management. I'd have to *do* and *say* the right things—identify the key **competencies** necessary to make things happen. After I lost my first four hires (and my *hot shit* attitude went away) I began to methodically break down the main things I'd spend my 10,000 hours on.

First, I had to learn how to *attract* and *hire* people.

It wasn't going to be okay for me to just sit back and wait for Tom to hire and assign them to me. It would be more beneficial if I selected my *own* people. Hence, I'd have to learn how to attract the right type of candidate. Developing and mastering a basic interview template (for first and second interviews), would be a priority. When I accomplished that, then I wouldn't be dependent on Tom or anyone else for the quality or quantity of my hires.

Then I had to build a *dependable* training system for the first three months.

From the outset it was painfully clear to me that the first 30, 60 and 90 days were most critical. I had already figured out that call reluctance was the Achilles heel of most salespeople. My first hires—the ones that had quit—did so because they didn't have the tools to handle failure and rejection. I reasoned that I'd have to spend the majority of my time during the first 30 days on two things:

1. **Making sure my agent's approach and front talk was rock solid:**

Competence breeds confidence. If they were confident in their skills they'd make more calls. I witnessed what happened when salespeople lost confidence or became confused. Their activity levels plummeted, and then they left.

2. Convincing them to remove emotion from their daily routine:

Showing them that all the pressure can be placed on the numbers, versus their shoulders. Within my first two months I figured out (with the help of my father), that the system works if you work it and that if you have solid skill-sets, then it's virtually all about managing the pipeline—keeping activity levels up.

In addition to learning the key competencies of hiring and on-boarding (by the way, we didn't call it "on-boarding" back then...I think we called it "trying to keep them around"), I was certain that I would have to personally develop a few key philosophies or *attitudes* about the training and management of salespeople. These would be the intangible paradigms, that when added to sound hiring and training skills, would actually make me a true leader of people versus just their assigned trainer or manager.

Becoming a true leader of people was very important to me, even at the very beginning of my sales management career. What I saw and experienced in Tom Smith was a person who knew how to really LEAD people. You followed Tom because he *connected* with you in a very individual way. You felt that he really understood what your internal motivations were. You followed Tom because he personally invested in your career. You didn't want to let him down. You trusted Tom. He did what he said he was going to do. Because of the high trust factor he had the influence to get you to think and behave differently.

I wanted to be a great leader, just like Tom, not just a mediocre manager, one that ruled by the *title* on my business card only. I quickly made a short list of the things that I thought set Tom apart from the rest of the crowd. These attributes would become the attitudes and values I would place the most emphasis on during my 10,000 hours.

The *responsibility* or *duty* of the leadership role:

I recognized that Tom felt a strong duty to get the best out of each person that made the commitment to come to work. I never heard Tom talk about his overrides. I never heard Tom say that a particular person was a "waste of time." Tom was focused on the person in front of him. It wasn't just about money to him. He said something really cool to me before I accepted the trainer promotion. He told me, "Joe, make sure you're doing this for the right reasons—because you want to impact the careers of others. Not just for the money." I knew that I would have to resolve that I truly wanted to lead others and impact lives, and I sincerely did. This would become my primary purpose—my WHY—for the balance of my career.

The ability to truly *connect* with people:

True connection yields incredible results when done right. The connection I'm referring to can be as simple as what Tom did with me early on. He spent a few minutes with me outside of the office asking me about my family, my parents, what kind of up-bringing I had experienced. He wanted to know what attracted me to outside sales and what my basic goals and objectives were. His questions indicated to me that he cared about me as a person and at the same time, my answers gave him a blueprint of how to coach and inspire me when I faced difficulties. He also asked me what my expectations were and he outlined his expectations.

Tom set the table for our relationship.

How (and when) to properly *invest* in others:

Tom made an impactful comment to me sometime early on in my leadership career. I never forgot it. It was after my third or fourth dude quit. I was ticked off because I had spent a great deal of time with that person. In fact, I'd spent more time with him than the prior three hires combined. I recall telling Tom how much potential this person had. He knew that my frustration level was through the roof, so he took me down the street for a beer. He lit up a cigarette, sipped his beer, and then calmly instructed, "Joe, you can never want this business for a person *more* than they want it for themselves." After that, I developed a paradigm for the way I invested in people for the balance of my leadership career, and it would always be in direct proportion to *their* investment.

Creating and articulating my *vision:*

Tom Smith helped me visualize a trajectory for my career. As a result, I was constantly striving to get to that next level. I always had something to reach for—look forward to. He had the ability to do the two things that can set a great leader apart from those that simply *manage*. First, Tom created a crystalized vision of where the team could go. Secondly, he did a masterful job of articulating and selling that vision to the team. I knew that if I could do those two things really well, I would have an edge over every other trainer or so-called leader.

By my third month of hiring and field training people, I had scratched out what would be my very first business plan. It was crude, but I had a mission and vision statement, some rudimentary goals, and had also outlined my leadership values and training initiatives. I drafted and re-drafted that plan several times and it actually started looking fairly professional. For the next twenty-four months, I focused on the best and most effective on-boarding practices I could identify. As a result, my retention got better and better. I also fixated on the values and attributes that would help me become a real leader of people. All of this work resulted in another promotion. I became a full charge sales manager in the spring of 1982. I wasn't a complete leader yet, but I felt I was getting closer.

One other significant, but invisible factor was also in play. Somewhere between the spring and summer of 1982 I had eclipsed the magical figure of my 10,000 hours.

As I reflect back on the hard work and struggles during my first three years in sales and sales management, I know now that this investment of time had quite a huge ROI attached to it and the returns would keep on giving for years. I didn't see it at the time, but those 10,000 hours had earned me a few things that were hard to even place a value on.

Freedom and Independence:

I could sell, on commission, without leads and also hire, train and retain salespeople. That skillset made me an incredibly marketable entity. I wasn't completely aware of it at the time, but those sought-after skills made it so I was reasonably free from control. In other words, I didn't have to work for any person or company that I didn't absolutely want to work for. I could go anywhere in my industry (or another) and make great money. The 10,000 hours made me a needed commodity. In addition, my self-governing nature enabled me to be far less dependent on fleeting external motivations or influences. The 10,000 hours had battle hardened me, making it possible for me to internalize some prodigious lessons and experiences.

I could stand on my own.

Self Confidence:

My 10,000 hours provided me with a great deal of confidence. I began to feel I belonged in the upper echelons. When I walked into a room, I felt I could hold my own with anyone in there. There was a confident strength about me that didn't exist before. I knew what I knew. I had a poise that only comes with the experience of being in the trenches and performing.

Think about Gladwell's theory for a moment. If you were sure you could become an expert at something if you practiced it for only 10,000 hours, but that craft would earn you relative freedom and independence for many years to come, would you do it—would you put in the hours?

Of course you would!

But then again, you're reading this book. (That means you are super smart!) We're talking about only investing 10,000 hours and then you'll have the tools, experience and confidence to forge a very fruitful and long career. Why wouldn't everybody simply dig in and do it—put in the hours? I'm still not sure of the answer to that question, even after close to forty years in leadership roles. Maybe the Pareto Principle is in play again.

I don't know, and honestly, I don't really care.

I simply know *what* I was instinctively willing to do—the price I was willing to pay. Those 10,000 hours were the foundation of me becoming a multi-millionaire and living a lifestyle that most people only dream of.

My 10,000 hours was a pretty small price to pay for all I've received. Don't you agree?

THE INCREDIBLE LESSONS

What can I say here? This chapter sort of hits you over the head with lessons; however, let me spend a moment to pull a few additional points from the original context for your deeper consideration.

✓ **Relative MASTERY takes time:**

Just like putting in the numbers when you're prospecting, you can't cheat this one either. For you to get really **competent** and **confident** at what you're doing, you gotta' **put in the time.** There's no shortcut. Sorry Millennials! (Just kidding, but I'm really not)

✓ **Just because you're good at ONE thing...:**

I had become a very good salesperson. So what. Those skill-sets live in a **different place** than the skill-sets required to hire, train and lead people. Every function requires slightly different **nuances**. Don't make the silly assumption that a role is going to be easy just because you were promoted to it. Don't go into something new with a ton of arrogance. This posture will **slow you down**. Go into a new role **COMMITTED** to **putting in your 10,000 hours**. The truth is, as you become more and more experienced at different elements of your business or industry, it probably won't take you all of 10,000 hours. However, act as if it will and then be pleasantly surprised when you arrive at mastery sooner.

✓ **Don't just PHONE IT IN:**

It will be easy for some readers to walk away from this chapter and think, "Cool. So if I just **hang out** for a few years I'll be really good at this gig, and be making great money." Wrong! I want to crush that myth. While showing up is half the battle, it's only **HALF** the battle. We have all heard the term "practice makes perfect," right? However, that's only true if you are practicing the **right** things! So what I did was very intuitive. I **outlined** the essential **competencies**, **attitudes** and **pipeline** practices I would spend my time working on. I began to break down and identify how I'd spend my 10,000 hours. I wasn't just *cruising* for three years, hoping for a lightening strike. I was **intentionally developing specific skill-sets** and mindsets.

✓ Take the LONG view:

I **did** and **didn't** know what I was doing. LOL!

What I **did** know is that I was heavily investing in myself so that I could move towards becoming a complete package. I eventually wanted to be considered an expert at my job. I knew I would have to **pay some sort of price** to become successful. Nobody was going to dump success in my lap. I'd have to work for each and every crumb—put in the hours. I did know that much.

What I **didn't** know was that this small price being paid to acquire the basic sales and leadership skills (and experience), would yield such an **exponential** return to me, and do so for such an extended period of time.

I had no conception of the massive returns on the 10,000 hours.

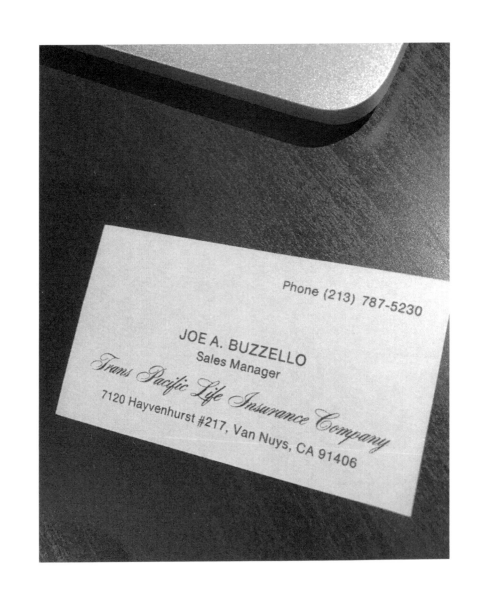

Phone (213) 787-5230

JOE A. BUZZELLO
Sales Manager

Trans Pacific Life Insurance Company

7120 Hayvenhurst #217, Van Nuys, CA 91406

CHAPTER SIXTEEN

The Parable of the Pullers

"Lessons of wisdom have the most power over us when they capture the heart through the groundwork of a story, which engages the passions."

—LAURENCE STERNE, Irish novelist

June Gloom is a weather condition in Los Angeles. It mostly occurs during the month of June, hence the name. There's this murky layer of soup in the sky that mysteriously doesn't burn off until some time after noon-ish. This strange San Fernando Valley weather condition seems to magically disappear around early July.

As June of 1982 loomed, things seemed pretty gloomy at Trans Pacific. There was a profound layer of murky soup hanging over the organization for sure. I had been recently promoted one more time and I now had a few trainers and a slew of agents under me. I was hiring as many people as possible, training them and trying like hell to retain them. My numbers were not bad at all, but that was only because I was overcompensating for the faltering economy by simply outworking every other sales manager around me. High interest rates, inflation and a lack of consumer confidence made it so that almost all of the small business people we sold to were suffering financially, hence our minor accident insurance plans became a much tougher sale.

To make matters worse, PennCorp hadn't revised their product line in years. They weren't keeping pace with the types of products business owners wanted. PennCorp was falling into the trap that Steve Jobs later made famous in a great little rant. Essentially (and I'm paraphrasing), Jobs suggested that when a company "stopped listening" to frontline salespeople and progressive product development people, they were screwed. When unenlightened C-suite execs defaulted to taking direction from the marketing department, or worse, "the financial guys," to make product related decisions, sales results always suffered. When we began voicing our opinion that it was getting more and more difficult to sell narrow scoped, low benefit policies, and we should be able to sell higher limits, they as much as said "shut up and sell the products that you have."

What worked for PennCorp in the '70s, wasn't at all working for them in the '80s!

The last part of this perfect storm of sales distractions was the removal of Bud and Norb as the agency directors of Trans Pacific. It happened quickly and quietly. We came in on a Monday and they were gone. When I peeked into their former office, all I saw was their two gigantic, ornate desks sitting there, with not a thing on them. All of the sales managers got the same memo from the home office in Santa Monica. It said something to the effect that, Bud Cole had "served the Trans Pacific division well, but has decided to seek another position and challenge within the PennCorp family." The same memo included the corporate-speak that, Mr. Norbert Cieslak had, "Elected to retire after a long and distinguished career," blah, blah, blah.

I'd been with PennCorp for three years and felt like a crusty old veteran, but in truth I was still only twenty-one years old and was trying to process those big changes and what they meant. I needed a sounding board, one that would help me ascertain the unvarnished truth. I found such a voice in one of the other Division Managers, a dude named Bill Cover. Normally, I would go to Tom Smith for feedback on an issue such as this, however, this time I opted not to. Tom was simply too polite. He was also the type of person that would sugar coat this scenario in order to protect my attitude. I wasn't interested in that kind of conversation. I wanted the raw version of the truth. I needed to talk to someone with an edge. Cover ran a small group of agents that sold life policies. Cover and his team weren't part of the mainstream Safe Drivers sales channel. They were a specialty product team and they mostly kept to themselves.

I originally befriended Cover because he seemed like he could broaden my view of things. He was a pot-smoking hippie from Ohio. He hid his face behind a full beard and an oversized pair of prescription sunglasses. Because he was a hippie, only truth came out of his mouth—and he hated "the man." On the morning after the memo came out, I grabbed a cup of coffee with him and one of his agents. The other agent, Marlene, was also a truth purveyor with zero filters. She was a sassy Japanese American from the west side of Los Angeles. The three of us had a rollicking discussion about Bud, Norb, the economy, our uncompetitive products, etc. Of course, Bill Cover and Marlene had taken a few more trips around the sun than I had, and as such, their cynical views could reduce anything down to precise observations and a few disparaging sound bites.

I was craving this.

"Look, this crap happens all the time in corporate America,"

Cover snorted. "Stanley Beyer and those fat cats in Santa Monica are looking at numbers on report. They don't want to hear excuses—the economy—outdated products—they don't give a shit about any of that. They just want numbers. And when the numbers don't happen, heads roll—someone gets blamed."

Marlene also had a brutally frank take on things.

"They instantly made the Trans Pacific division more profitable by blowing out those two buffoons. What the f__k did Bud and Norb add to the mix anyway? Bud walked around with his bad toupee, barking at people. And Norb...useless as tits on a bull. All they care about in Santa Monica is shareholder value. They don't give a rat's ass about anything else. Now, at least they don't have to pay 'Big Foot' and 'Mr. Useless' inflated salaries and bonuses."

If I wanted a matter-of-fact opinion of things, I was getting it.

It was actually refreshing and it gave me my first exposure to what *jaded* actually sounds like. Again, I could have gone to Tom, but he would have poured some sugar on it—trying to protect my fragile psyche. I asked Cover and Marlene what they thought would happen next. Would they close Trans Pacific? Would they promote someone from within? They both were of the mind that as long as Santa Monica could squeeze a profit out of the Trans Pacific division, the doors would remain open. Cover thought that PennCorp would most likely be sending someone up from the home office to run the agency on an interim basis. The big office sat empty for the next three weeks while we all plodded along doing our jobs.

As the clock struck July 1st, a sunny new face showed up in the big office and the murky soup cleared away.

Months before, as the numbers at the Trans Pacific division began to falter, Stanley Beyer and his C-suite crew engaged an outside consultant to tell them what to do. Unbeknownst to me, this consultant had been poking around for a while. He had spent some time with Bud and Norb and had also rode along for a day in the field with several of the more tenured sales managers. Apparently, part of the consultant's final recommendations included the removal of both Bud and Norb from their positions, which was a recommendation Stanley didn't argue with. It seemed as if the stock jockeys in Santa Monica were so impressed with the outside consultant, they offered him a contract to go run Trans Pacific for a while.

The dude's name was Don Widell. He was a dignified, soft-spoken semi-retired businessman, who had cashed out, then became bored and started his own consulting firm. I met him on that first Monday in July when he walked into my small office area, sat down at my desk and smiled at me. He stuck out his hand and said, "Hello, Joe. I've heard a lot of good things about you."

So at this point I'd been in sales or sales leadership for four years, including the stint in the car business. All of my friends were graduating, or starting their Master's programs. In my own way of thinking, I had completed my four-year degree, except it was a sheepskin in sales and sales management. I was about to experience another one of those aha moments—an epiphany. It would be one that would lay the groundwork for my imaginary Master's degree. Don Widell would dispense this lesson in a dark corner of the Van Nuys Airport bar. The message I'd receive from him would upset the order of importance I'd previously placed on the finer aspects of recruiting and sales training.

I would never forget it.

Don gathered all of the sales managers together for a discussion about what *was* working and *wasn't* working. Ironically, we met at the same airport bar that Larry Story and I parked our butts in when we learned our damn scripts three years earlier. Appetizers and cocktails were vacuumed up like none of us had ever seen free food or drinks before. There was lots of friendly small talk, and then Don began to turn the conversation towards business. He made it abundantly clear that we could "speak openly" about things—everything would be "off the record" and there would be "no judgment." Tom Smith leaned over and whispered in my ear. He suggested that I might want to "be careful" with what I said. Just as he was telling me that, the floodgates opened up. Managers that hadn't been heard from in years spoke up. They finally had a chance to mouth off and have their voices heard. Of course, as most of these *off the record* discussions go, the conversation quickly degenerated into a bitch session. Most of the complaints centered around how bad the economy was, and how obsolete our products had become.

Don was skilled at listening carefully and then redirecting the conversation. He challenged us to shift our focus away from the things we had no control over, such as the economy. He also acknowledged that our current product line had not kept pace with competitors and noted that it was something that PennCorp was in the process of reviewing. Then he moved the conversation towards the factors we did have some direct control over.

Several of the managers (including myself), had commented on how much time we spent recruiting, interviewing and field training people. We added that most of these salespeople would eventually leave anyway. I was probably spending more time than most trying to fine-tune my interview process. I became obsessed with shiny new interview questions and techniques. I'd started to believe that a more careful selection of candidates would help me find the *right* people. Some of us had also fallen into the rabbit hole of pushing out more training. We rationally deduced that more training would help us retain a higher percentage of agents. If we just spent more time with them, then we'd have better results, right? As a consequence of sales numbers going down, we all became mad scientists. We tried to perfectly identify (up front), who was going to make it—who'd be worth our time to train—and then we'd spend MORE time with each of those hires.

It wasn't working.

Worse...it was actually having the opposite effect. As our total number of hires went down and we spent mountains of time with people we were convinced were going to be stars, our emotional and physical gas tanks were slowly heading towards empty. Don listened to us intently, absorbing our diatribes. When most of the sales managers got done dumping (and we were on our third round of cocktails), Don calmly cleared his throat and began to speak.

Don gave us his back-story. He was a three-sport athlete at a small college in Washington State. After that, he enlisted into the service and served in Korea. When he returned from military service he started a small business out of his garage. He humbly began by selling a line of pots and pans door-to-door with a small sales team. Eventually, his business grew and he relocated into larger facilities. By the time he was in his forties, he controlled a sizeable corporate enterprise with a large national sales force. The name of the company was Cordon Bleu Cookware.

His story centered on the difficulties his company experienced at one juncture. Many years earlier, the company's sales started to flat line. Don was the best salesperson the company had, but due to their massive growth, he'd become ensnared into the role of CEO. He had no choice but to delegate the sales channel to others and trust they would continue to drive numbers the way he had.

Don's sales management team convinced him that resources should be directed to the *profiling* of all potential new hires with aptitude and suitability tests, so he spent a ton of money on these tests for them. Next, his sales managers convinced him to build out a more complex training process. They wanted more and better training for each and every salesperson hired. Don acquiesced and spent time and money on outside trainers to revamp their on-boarding protocols. However, it seemed that the more money they spent on areas such as candidate selection and complex training models, the worse new sales results became. Don leaned back in his chair at the bar that night, poured himself a brew, relating the following story like he was the camp counselor and we were scouts around the fire, toasting up some marshmallows.

What followed was one of the greatest nuggets I've ever received!

"I was sitting on my couch one Saturday afternoon," he told us. "I was watching ABC's Wide World of Sports. I was mentally preoccupied—at a crossroads with my company—worrying a great deal about how to turn sales around. Jim McKay was doing an introduction of an event ABC was covering that day. Each year in March, people and dogs from around the world converge on the state of Alaska to take part in what has become known as the 'Last Great Race' on the planet, the *Iditarod*. The race began in 1973. It's a thousand mile endurance test for the mushers and the dogs that run its course."

The winner that year was a man from Willmar, Minnesota, Rick Swenson. Rick went on to win a total of five Iditarod events and eventually became known as the "King of the Iditarod." Don told us that he became more interested in what was on his television screen when the reporter shoved a microphone in the face of the tired champion.

Don continued weaving his story.

"The man conducting the interview asked a few questions about the weather and course conditions, then he asked his last question. It turned out to be a doozy. The interviewer probed, 'I'm sure our viewers at home want to know how you *train* your dogs. How do you train all of those dogs so well each year?'"

I noticed that Don hesitated a few seconds before continuing his anecdote. He was checking to see who was listening and who wasn't. The other guys seemed more interested in their cocktails than the story, but I could tell that the story was important to Don and, at the very least, he'd drawn me into his web.

"So, Rick Swenson looks at the ABC interviewer like the guy has a screw loose. The champion cocks his head and replies, 'Sir, I don't TRAIN dogs. I'm not a dog trainer. I hook dogs up to the sled and I look for the PULLERS. I keep the pullers and work with them. I release the rest.'"

"I hook dogs up to the sled and I look for the PULLERS. I keep the pullers and work with them. I release the rest."

Don stopped talking, leaned back and smiled. I did a quick 180. None of my colleagues seemed to be listening that intently to what he had to say. One of the other managers had even left to take a bathroom break.

Don Continued.

"I jumped off the couch when the winner made this statement. It hit me like a ton of bricks. Spending more money and time trying to pick the perfect candidate or wasting corporate resources to revamp training wasn't going to change our sales results at all. I realized we'd gotten off course; we'd been focusing on the WRONG things. I knew right then and there that I'd need to get back into the field and refocus our leadership team, get them thinking differently."

Don went on to explain that when his company was growing sales by leaps and bounds, they didn't have sophisticated interviewing techniques and didn't even have any fancy classroom training. It was just Don and a few other guys in the field, having fun and working with the people that were ready to run hard along side of them.

"We didn't have time to waste with anyone that wasn't ready to go to work," Don stated. "We released them. We let them go. We simply identified and worked with the PULLERS!"

After Don experienced his own little couch epiphany that afternoon, he got back into the field and redirected the paradigm of his organization. He challenged sales leadership to move away from BS theories that were NEVER going to be productive. He came to believe that selection and training processes are overrated if you don't look for the *pullers* and redirect your focus on them. He asked his sales leaders to look into the hearts and minds of their sales people. Don challenged them to identify and engage with those that were ready to run hard. He implored them to *connect to* and *invest in* those people and help them get what they wanted. He then suggested that they gently *release* the rest—learn how to fail obvious failures much faster in their system. Don taught them to NOT spend their precious time trying to convince a person to do something (sales), that they weren't ready to do.

Of course, there's always the rest of the story.

Don told us that the paradigm shift caused his company's sales and revenues to skyrocket. The company then posted strong double-digit increases quarter after quarter and year after year. A few years later a large conglomerate made an offer and bought the company. Don and his partners became multi-multi millionaires as a result of the sale.

Don's story made quite an impression on me that night. I started thinking about what my recruiting and selection process had become. I was trying to *cherry pick* the winners using aptitude tests and complex interview techniques. Both tools were unreliable. In addition, I was spending *equal* field time with each new salesperson, trying to be *fair*. I was training each and every new salesperson the same way, investing the same amount of time with everyone. That wasn't working either. You can educate a sales person until you're blue in the face, but if they're not ready to put in the hours, then all you have is an unmotivated professional student.

After absorbing this incredible story, I began looking for the *pullers*. I hired everyone that I thought would represent our brand well, however, I didn't invest in each of them equally and blindly. I started taking notice of specific factors. I began to spend prime field time with *only* those that were willing to do the work now—people that had heart and grit to get the job done.

Don's story and his lesson was so powerful to me that I eventually started re-telling it to people that were becoming leaders. My mantra became "If you LIKE a person, and you think they're coachable, give them a chance. If they go to work alongside of you—if they're a puller—then great...keep working with them. If they are not ready to go to work, release them—or, at least, don't spend your prime time with them."

That night began the transition from my basic degree to my advanced degree in sales and leadership. Don's story captivated my mind and heart that night. The lesson and the wisdom dispensed that evening would not soon wear off; in fact, it would become the basis of my hiring and training philosophies for many years to come.

I finished my beer, thanked Don for his time and drove home.

As for the other guys sitting in the dark corner of that stupid airport bar in Van Nuys on that night in 1982...I think some of them may still be sitting there, complaining about how hard it is to find and train salespeople, never having really heard Don's lesson.

THE INCREDIBLE LESSONS

Don dumped a ton of nuggets on me that night. Let's unpack them.

✓ **When the 'C-suite' stops LISTENING, the end is near:**

Penn Corp and their subsidiaries slowly became **dinosaurs** in the insurance industry. This happened because they stopped listening. When the C-suite becomes **arrogant** and **shuts down** to great ideas from the troops, you can mark that as **the beginning of the END** and you should blow the dust off of your resume.

It's not going to get better.

✓ **NUMBERS usually trump PEOPLE in corporate America:**

In my humble opinion, nothing about this has changed over the years. Maybe changes are made in a more *gentrified* manner today, but don't mistake it, when shareholder or equity partner value is at risk, heads will roll. Bud and Norb were **sacrificial lambs**, but also they made themselves **easy targets**. Ultimately, they were easy to get rid of because they were highly compensated, but actually provided **little tangible value** to those they served. **People are quite expendable** when numbers suck. They always have been, they always will be. When the bottom line is grim, you gotta' pretend to be doing something to fix it, right? Firing people is the easiest thing to do.

For this reason, you should never be **confused** as to what your level of **importance** or **value** actually is to a corporation. You'd be wise to always have an **updated resume** handy... and also have many, many **good industry CONTACTS!** You want to stay **agile** and **connected**. If you cocoon *only* in your bubble, with your head down, it is a dangerous corner to paint yourself into.

✓ **PEERS are usually more HONEST and unfiltered than your hierarchy:**

When I sat with Bill Cover and Marlene, they had **no agenda**. They didn't override me like Tom Smith did. They had *no dog in the fight*. Bill and Marlene didn't have to worry about protecting my fragile emotional state, because it wasn't connected to their pocketbook. They could **speak openly**.

What I learned is that honest (down in the dirt) conversations with peers can be very REVEALING. These types of **unfiltered exchanges** can give you **different perspectives** on things. You simply have to make sure that these dialogs don't degrade into conversations that are negative, for the sake of being negative.

✓ **STORIES have incredible TEACHING power:**

How is it that I can recollect the vivid details about Bud telling me to go purchase *Think and Grow Rich*, or my Chilidog Epiphany, or Don's Iditarod story? My wife, Beth, is always amazed at the details of long lost conversations we've had, that I can recall perfectly. In most cases, the reason I can recall rich detail is that they're *wrapped* in the blanket of a memorable story or experience—something that touched me emotionally. I'm talking *right brain* here. This is supposedly the part of our brains that is impressed by **EMOTIONAL** experiences. Stories and experiences **stick** with us. Left brain stuff like, facts, data and logic, can quickly leak out of our brain and ears.

✓ **You can LEAD a horse to water...:**

Or should I say, "You can hook a dog up to the sled!" LOL! What I took away from Don's story that night is that we often focus a great deal of time and money screening, hiring, on-boarding, training, etc., before we simply identify **what's in their heart**. In other words, we fail to identify if they are ready to **DO THE WORK now**—run along side of us.

I actually invested the time to talk to Don extensively about how his philosophies and strategies morphed after his Iditarod epiphany. Specifically, I asked him what changed for him after watching that Wide World of Sports episode. Bottom line, he **increased the *volume*** of people they interviewed, and **decreased** the time and money spent trying to make *'right' selections*. Then, they **decreased** the time and money spent purely in the *classroom*, and **increased** the time a trainer spent *in the FIELD* with a new salesperson.

He also mentioned that they *expedited* the first field experience for their new hire. (They moved that timeline up) He determined that there was no better way to **filter** or **gauge** a person's willingness to get bloody than to get them in the field to see their reaction to the actual type and volume of work. They also worked on *failing obvious failures fast*. They established much **shorter time intervals** for the minimum activity and result expectations.

Everything Don said to me was brilliant then...and it's brilliant now. The reasons I believe this is borderline *genius thinking* for leaders is that we are ultimately only looking for people that are "pullers." So why not **focus all of your efforts up front** to figuring out who's READY to pull your sled now? It occurs to me that **all of the other stuff is wasted motion** and emotion.

✓ **When the student is READY, the teacher will APPEAR:**

By now you may be sensing a subtle theme in terms of the unique way I've been able to learn my craft. While it's true that I've been blessed to have many mentors of varied shapes and sizes enter my life; you still have to be *ready* to receive their message **when they SHOW UP**. When I sat listening to Don tell that cool dog sled racing story that night, I glanced around the bar. You'll recall that I mentioned that some of my fellow managers were **not actively listening**. I WAS listening...intently.

My lack of *formal* education may have something to do with how aggressively and intently **I searched for knowledge**. I've made a whole career out of thinking that I may be *the dumbest guy* **in the room**. This is a good thing. If you get to a place where you feel like you've "arrived" or that you know far more about your craft than almost anybody, well... you're kind of screwed.

Really great people, with really great things to say may cross your path, but you won't see or hear them if you think you are the *smartest* person in the room.

CHAPTER SEVENTEEN

Jumping The Shark

"The first responsibility of a leader is to define reality."
—MAX DE PREE, author

I walked away from Don Widell's fireside chat a more enlightened person.

His passion for leadership was obvious as he reached out to the group of sales managers that evening a few months earlier. He got us to open up and tell him what was on our minds. He was there to help us and to try to get our agency turned around. He was a good man and watching him in action made me want to become an even better leader and entrepreneur. My batteries were recharged temporarily, however, as I returned to my daily routine over the following weeks, I continued to encounter those things I could not change.

The economy was brutal, but I knew it would cycle back around. The factor that really continued to kill us were those damn outdated products, the old plans that PennCorp refused to spend time and money on and revise. In addition to that, the claims department started slow paying our claimants. The comment that really hit me like a sledgehammer came from the long time office operations manager. I was asking her to call Santa Monica and find out why a simple accident claim wasn't being processed and she asked, "Why do you have your panties in a wad? You get your commission check on time each week. Isn't that the only thing you salespeople really care about?"

I remember walking out of the office that day and going straight to Studio City Golf Course. I hit two large buckets of balls on the range and drained a beer. It was only 1:30 p.m. in the afternoon, but I couldn't face a prospect or one of my team members.

The culture at Trans Pacific and PennCorp had changed.

Not for the better.

Rather irrevocably.

And Don Widell wasn't going to save it.

A few days after the "panties in a wad" comment I was in the break room when Bill Cover walked in. Cover and I had started to spend more time together in the previous months. He was becoming a valuable sounding board for me. He was massaging his bushy beard and wolfing down an apple fritter as I approached him.

"How you doing with all of this?" he inquired.

We were the only two people in the room, so I didn't filter. I told him that my head was screwed up, I was starting to dislike the work and I didn't have the energy to fake it for much longer. He nodded his head in an understanding way and blurted out, "Nobody with any talent is going to stay around here very long, and you, my young friend, have real talent."

With that little comment, he squeezed my shoulder and walked out of the room. As if on cue, Marlene, who had quickly become our third wheel for offsite happy hours, walked in.

"What's shakin' good lookin'?"

She gave me a little hug and poured some black coffee in her Journey mug as she lit up her morning Virginia Slim.

"I don't know, Marlene. I wish I could tell you that everything's good. But it's not. I just told Cover, my gas tank is kind of empty."

She set down her mug and glared at me through her Coke bottle glasses and then dumped. "Look, you know we're not going to stay around this place, right? The handwriting's on the wall. The products are shit, the home office is shit, they've run the course and all the good ones in this agency are gonna' leave."

Her diatribe continued for another two or three minutes. She advocated her philosophies about corporate America, how screwed up it all is and how Santa Monica doesn't "give a crap" about anything except profits. She told me that from her experience, smart people in sales "take care of their own business" and they know when to "get off a tired horse and find a fresh one."

"Look, you're not stupid," she told me. "But you're gonna' suffer from loyalty. You won't leave until your buddy Tom Smith tells you to leave, and that will be a mistake because this place is a f____n' dead end."

She snuffed out her cigarette in somebody else's empty coffee cup.

"Do me a favor...call Cover later and make a time to get with him. He'll tell you where we're headed. We're blowing this taco stand— we're only waiting for our pending commission checks to clear." She gave me a sweet little peck on the cheek and whispered, "Don't be the last one standing on the deck of the Titanic."

Marlene winked, walked out and I didn't see her again at Trans Pacific.

I heard Cover's original message, and Marlene's subsequent sermon loud and clear. Marlene was right; I was suffering from a *loyalty* thing. Tom had told me to "sit tight and wait things out" but unless he knew something that I didn't know, that advice was starting to sound like "find a high part of the boat and you and I can be the last two to drown."

There were also the rampant rumors that PennCorp was for sale. Those rumors had circulated for most of the three years I was with them, but lately insiders in Santa Monica had substantiated that they weren't just rumors anymore. When I met with Cover and other managers that I learned were leaving, they all pretty much educated me on the same theory. What Cover, Marlene and others were all telling me was that when things go bad in an organization, they rarely *reverse* themselves, and if they do, it takes a damn long time. In a side-bar conversation with Marlene, she acerbically stated, "When you take the 'L' out of Lover, it's over." Of course, she was referring to relationships, but the same philosophy could easily be applied to a business or sales organization. The bottom line was, things were bad. Hence, I'd have to make a decision to stay or go, and then live with the consequences.

Later in my business career I read about an idiom called, "jumping the shark." This phrase was popularized by radio personality Jon Hein in the 1980s. The saying is based on an episode aired during the fifth-season of Happy Days. It's about the scene where Fonzie jumps over a shark while on water skis. The whole thing was deemed a ratings ploy because the premise was so detached from the original storyline of the sitcom. It was as if the producers and writers had no new ideas, believed the show to be past its peak, and were desperate to keep the show relevant.

In the beginning, the phrase was explicitly used within the entertainment industry, describing an episode of a television show where there was a stunt or improbable scene written in—a scenario that would be regarded as a fraught attempt to keep viewers' interest. Therefore, scenes labeled "jumping the shark" were considered indications that the show had drifted irreversibly from a proven blueprint.

Jumping the Shark was subsequently broadened into the mainstream vernacular to include scenarios where a company or brand's effort's declined or shifted so drastically that it becomes unrecognizable or unwelcome.

What Cover, Marlene and others were telling me is that Trans Pacific and PennCorp had "jumped the shark." PennCorp had peaked and was now on a sharp decline, and things would NOT get any better.

It was my job as a young entrepreneur to define the reality of it all, but it wasn't a stretch to do that, because the whole Trans Pacific thing just didn't feel right in my gut anymore. I had started to trust my gut instinct more and more as I matured. My intuition told me that I was stuck in the wrong place. Ultimately, that was all I needed to push me over the edge and decide to move on. This would be a prudent decision, as PennCorp would never put a dime into the Trans Pacific division. They'd simply let the loyal people who stayed there wither away on the vine.

My current gig had *jumped the shark* for sure. It was time to follow the smart guys out the door and grab a lifeboat, while there were still some available.

*   *   *

I followed what occurred with PennCorp after I left.

I'm the curious sort—fascinated with organizational development, and even more so with organizational decline. PennCorp would eventually sell out to a company called American Can. Stanley Beyer and the others got their big juicy cash and stock payouts, but as I later learned from my digging, there had been some good old-fashioned book-cooking going on in Santa Monica. Apparently, the bad financial behavior had been happening for years and years.

The chief bean counter (CFO) of PennCorp had shifted ledger entries between their underlying companies so creatively that back in July of 1974 the local Securities and Exchange Commission office (SEC) filed a complaint and injunction against them. The complaint named Stanley Beyer along with some other key executives. The investigation report was pretty humorous to read. Amongst a host of allegations, PennCorp was concealing transactions in order to enhance the financial statements of the parent company. These transactions enabled certain partners to take amounts into revenue, which they otherwise couldn't do rendering PennCorp filings as *false* in not disclosing these matters. Finally, the complaint alleged that, between 1969 and 1971, the individual executive defendants, sold quantities of their personally held Pennsylvania Life Co. stock while possessing gobs of material inside information. Beyer, and the others eventually consented to the entry of a final judgment of permanent injunction.

In today's hypersensitive white-collar crime environment, they'd all be somebody's *bitch* in a federal penitentiary; however, they all got off with a slap on the wrist. Years later, they were able to sell their company at a hefty price. We were all simply tiny cogs in their ongoing wheel, killing ourselves day-in and day-out on the street, selling those $39.00 accident plans while Stanley Beyer and the others got rich, moving numbers from one column entry to another, illegally, legally, who really cares.

Ain't that America?

All I knew was that in the summer of 1982, PennCorp had jumped the shark and I made the decision that I wouldn't be the last dude standing there on the deck of the Titanic with a finger up my nose.

I guess that I'd gotten what I wanted and needed out of my first four years in the real world. I had completed my imaginary Bachelor's Degree in sales and sales leadership. It was time for me to begin my informal *Master's Degree*, and that experience would come at a very expensive price. During the next five years I'd become a *product* of what I read, and even more importantly, whom I'd made the choice to associate with.

Unfortunately, I didn't choose the later very carefully.

(To be continued in Volume II)

Too Many People to Thank

"People trying to reach goals succeed at a much greater rate if they're connected to a strong human support system."

—DR. HENRY CLOUD, author, behavioral psychologist

I'm certainly that...*connected* to a strong human support system.

Between my family, close friends, mentors, colleagues, and the core followers of the work I do, there are way too many people to thank.

But when we write another book we must always try, right?

To the many kind followers and supporters of the work; each and every time I receive a text, ping, IM, email or comment from you, I smile. The strong platform of subscribers that we've built over the last four years has been surprising, and just plain wonderful. I am so thankful for all of the people that tell me that they receive value from what I put out there. When somebody lets me know that something we've taught, or something I said was "life changing," well...there just isn't anything better!

So first and foremost, a GIANT thanks to all the core subscribers and supporters of the work!

As you are now aware, my life in sales has been full of mentors, saints and sinners. I'll even thank the sinners (and criminals), but I'll focus more on the mentors and saints mentioned in this volume. A big shout out and *thanks* to the wacky crew at Universal Ford for an unlikely first experience in sales. Be you dead or alive (in some cases, I just don't know) I'd like to thank Serge, Frankie, Jackman, Miker, Boegner and Bugelli and all the rest. You guys helped me break the seal, and you performed some world-class stupid human tricks, never to be duplicated!

My unlikely experience working for the Trans Pacific division of PennCorp was more respectable than pushing tin cans for Universal Ford, but it was just as entertaining. Bud and Norb were actually capable agency managers. As much as I make fun of Norb (because he kinda' WAS stealing a paycheck), I still learned a few things from him. Bud was a damn force of nature. He got me reading books. For that ONE thing, I will be eternally grateful to him. The cast of characters at Trans Pacific was as rich as you can imagine. I didn't have enough pages in this volume to mention all of them, but I'm so thankful that Bill Darnell, Larry Story, Don Widell, John Jamelkowski, Bill Cover and Marlene Myoshi were part of my life in sales. The later two, Cover and Marlene, will play a continued role in my career.

Stay tuned for Volume II!

Of course, I'm not sure I would have become the sales professional that I did without the guiding hand of Mr. Tom Smith. Tom

Smith and his wonderful wife, Sylvia, are retired and living in the state of Washington at the time of this writing. Tom and I lost touch many years back, but there isn't a week that goes by that I don't think about him, and smile. When he was at the top of his game, there was nobody better.

It has become routine for me to ask a few people (I should say, "bug" a few people) to do a "test read" of the early draft of my manuscript. I do this to get *real* and *unfiltered* input. The raw comments that come back cause me to revise and rewrite. I did sucker a few people into this and I received some great input. My thanks to Les Heinsen, Jack Holder, Aaron Dunnill, Rich Kunz and Jody Willis. These people were kind enough to be honest with me.

There are also all of those very important and busy people that I bugged and bugged to "take a read" on the finished manuscript for testimonial purposes. I'm going to reel off the names, and I hope that I captured them all, as some of the reviews and testimonials are still arriving to our office at the time of this writing.

A big giant "Thanks" goes out to: Alex Bayer, Jeb Blount, Bob Burg, Bill Cates, Marc Emmer, Doug Fox, Andy Glaub, John Grubbs, Les Heinsen, Jason Hill, Jack Holder, Tony Iannarino, Bill Leider, Tim Martin, Adam Michaels, Tony Parinello, S. Renee, Chad Schneider, Paul Schween, Eric Silverman, Leeza Steindorf, Gary Ware, Jeff West & Dr. Tommy Watson. These are all really gifted authors, speakers, trainers, coaches or entrepreneurs, except for Gary Ware. I'm so appreciative that they took their valuable time to offer an endorsement of this work.

We don't want to forget the unsung heroes of a good-looking book! I am always so happy to be able to hand over my (almost) finished work to Jerry Dorris and his great team at AuthorSupport.com. They do such a great job with the cover concept and all of the interior design elements and industry standard formatting.

Thanks so much Jerry and staff!

Okay...my family.

My mother and father had such an incredible impact on my life that nothing I accomplish happens without their imprint. My mother relentlessly counseled me that I could "do anything I set my mind to" and that the "love of Jesus, and the example of his life" would always be there for me to draw strength from. I'm not sure I always understood her weighty spiritual comments, especially when I was indestructible, but I sure as heck understand what she was talking about now.

My father, Buzz, was my rock—my hero—my buddy. He wasn't here on this planet long enough. I see his face and hear his voice everyday. I will see him and mom again one day.

Beth and I recently relocated to Scottsdale, Arizona. We love it here. It's a perfect place to live for us. (Except during July and August... LOL...like a damn pizza oven!) One of the great benefits of moving back here is that I get to spend a lot more time with my big sister, Regina. She lives here. There's nobody like her—a classic—heart of gold. Regina has always been my biggest protector and cheerleader. I want to thank her for being those two things. Also...she's smarter than me. She's also an expert salesperson—but I never trained her. Not sure where she got that talent.

I always strive to make her proud of me.

I'm not sure our daughter, Alyssa, has read any of my books so far. I'm not even sure people from Generation Z even know how to read! LOL! She certainly doesn't seem very interested in this book, other than to make fun of the very bad suite I'm wearing on the cover. Maybe the whole thing is one big act. Perhaps she secretly reads my work and loves it!

A father can only dream.

Anyway, what a wonderful and brilliant girl she is, and she is the love of my life. I try to do things to make her proud of me too.

My wife is really, really pretty and really, really smart. I know... hard to believe I snagged a good-looking smart chic. But I did!

Beth took a large role in the production of this book. She became my *primary* editor, offering me some great structural advice. Her keen insight made this book better. In addition to all of her tireless editing work, she offers that one critical thing that any creative person like me needs.

She talks me off the ledge.

I don't know of an author who hasn't written a manuscript and then (at least once), said, "This is crap and nobody will read it!" Hence, her gentle nudge—her sweet, soft voice telling me how "solid" the content is, and how people will "love it" and "take great value away from the book."

That's the secret sauce. That's the one thing that gets a book finished—confirmation that the work is *good* enough.

I can't thank Beth enough. I love her so much.

Okay.

Like I said, I'm certainly *connected* to a strong human support system. I'm quite blessed. Good, bad and ugly, I've learned from them all. They've supplied the unlikely experiences, and provided the incredible lessons. Too many people of all kinds to thank in my life, be they family friends, mentors, advisors, colleagues, teammates, followers of the work, saints, detractors, attackers, sinners, reprobates and, oh...the criminals.

(In Volume II you'll meet a few more criminals!)

The Incredible Lessons

CHAPTER TEN: Breaking The Seal

CHAPTER ELEVEN: Spaghetti Logic

CHAPTER TWELVE: Read and Grow Rich

If you enjoyed the content and lessons in this book, then please go over to **www.JoeBuzzello.com**

Please leave your first name and best email address and **register this book**. Joe will send you a coaching program as a **complimentary gift**!

In 2018 Joe founded **SEL Source Thought Partners**. This platform serves as a mentorship community for **Sales** professionals, **Entrepreneurs** and **Leaders**.

SEL Source ON-DEMAND is an exclusive membership site that gives our followers 24/7 ACCESS to all of Joe's new and archived content and also the content of all of the SEL Source affiliates.

To learn more about SEL Source ON-DEMAND, please go to:

www.SELsource.com

67842163R00107

Made in the USA
Columbia, SC
02 August 2019